SLOW LOSS

A MEMOIR OF MARRIAGE
UNDONE BY DISEASE

SLOW LOSS

LOIS KELLY

Copyrighted Material

Slow Loss: A Memoir of Marriage Undone by Disease

Copyright © 2024 by Lois E. Kelly. All Rights Reserved.

No part of this publication may be reproduced, stored in a retrieval system or transmitted, in any form or by any means—electronic, mechanical, photocopying, recording or otherwise—without prior written permission from the publisher, except for the inclusion of brief quotations in a review.

For information about this title contact the publisher:

Foghound
www.foghound.com
lkelly@foghound.com

ISBNs:
978-0-9963137-3-5 (softcover)
978-0-9963137-4-2 (eBook)

Printed in the United States of America

Cover art: Lois Kelly
Cover design: Logica Design
Interior design: 1106 Design

To Greg:
You saw the best in all of us

CONTENTS

INTRODUCTION: A Portrait of Marriage Amid Dementia and Grief — xi

BEFORE — 1
    The Prom Party — 3
    Fudge Cake and Death Marches — 9
    Morning Walks — 13
    Missed Signs — 15
    Death and Dying Years — 19
    Family Changes: The Lost Son — 23

DURING: THE EARLY YEARS — 29
    Coming Out as a Fraud — 31
    Mr. Perseverance's First Tour of Duty — 37
    The Plot Changes — 47

DURING: 2019 — 49
    The Voice — 51
    Sometimes When Listening — 53

SLOW LOSS

    Out-of-Control Impulse Control   57

DURING: 2020   61

    Evil House Spirits   63
    Storm after Storm   69
    Put the Dog Down   73
    Help   79
    Fairies Need to Fly   83

DURING: 2021   87

    Time to Go   89
    What About the Sons?   93
    The Mafia Don   95
    Enraged by Perky Advice   99
    Name Every Sign   103
    Please, Please, Please   105

DURING: 2022   109

    A Spring All-Nighter   111
    Distract Me, Loves   117
    The POW Signs In   119
    His Big Break   125
    I Look at the Picture of the Gun   133
    Making a Move   137
    Truly Pissed   141
    Loneliness is an Orange Dust Mop   145
    St. John Blesses Me   149

DURING: 2023   155

    The Wall of Pictures   157

CONTENTS

I Am Falling Apart, Thank You for Asking   163
The Dying Manatee   167
Everything Is in Order and Other Lies   177
My Big Fat Portuguese Death Vigil   179

AFTER: 2023-2024   187

The Lost Summer   189
The Boys' Club: A Psychedelic Journey Through Grief   193
Goodbye to That Woman   203
Egg Fights and Ice Queens   209
A Fatty Betrayal   211
Living in the Land of Liminality   215

ACKNOWLEDGMENTS   219
ABOUT THE AUTHOR   223

INTRODUCTION

A Portrait of Marriage
Amid Dementia and Grief

When I said my marriage vows forty years ago, I tripped over the words "for richer or poorer." My family laughed because we are all world-class money worriers. My husband and I didn't obsess about money until the end when we spent huge amounts on his health.

The hardest vows to honor were "in sickness and health." If I had known how difficult it would be to be married to someone with a twelve-year (at least) degenerative brain disease (Parkinson's), I might have fled the church like Elaine in the final scene of the movie *The Graduate*.

Some books about living with and caring for a spouse are filled with wondrous love and everlasting devotion. Anyone who has lived with someone with dementia, Alzheimer's, Lewy body dementia, Parkinson's disease, or any other long-haul degenerative neurological disease will call bullshit on those sweet and saccharine tales.

SLOW LOSS

Based on my experience and that of my caregiver friends, losing our partners cognitively, emotionally, and physically over a long period is like lingchi, a Chinese term that means "slow slicing."

We wonder what crisis is going to happen next; we're always on alert for the worst. We beat ourselves up thinking we should be more patient or kinder. We shame ourselves for wishing for our partners to die because we, too, are starting to lose our minds. We scream or repress our rage as we wonder if life will ever be "normal" again. We envy those couples growing old together and then admonish ourselves for doing so. Of course, we want people to be happy. And yet, why couldn't that have been our life too?

In his book *Faith, Hope, and Carnage*, Australian musician Nick Cave reflects on loss: "Sometimes you find a grieving person constricted around the thing they have lost; they've become ossified and impossible to penetrate. Other people go the other way and grow open and expansive."

This book is about the slow, slicing loss I experienced as I became more caregiver than wife and how I survived and evolved into someone different. During the last four years of my husband's twelve-year disease, I thought I had permanently ossified into a bitchy ice queen and would never again be optimistic, creative, and of the world.

This book is a collection of defining stories as a wife before my husband's disease, as a reluctant caregiver, and as a widow filled with enormous relief and uneasy grief. Each chapter is a short story of how I coped, lost my mind, found solace in unexpected ways, and eventually began to heal.

The most valuable and reassuring wisdom I've heard about gradually losing a spouse to a degenerative neurological disease is that great love and great suffering transform us.

INTRODUCTION

"Only love and suffering are strong enough to break down our usual ego defenses, crush our dualistic thinking, and open us to Mystery," writes Fr. Richard Rohr in his book *The Naked Now: Learning to See as the Mystics See*. "In my experience, they, like nothing else, exert the mysterious chemistry that can transmute us from a fear-based life into a love-based life. None of us are exactly sure why."

This is a story of how I broke and opened. This is a story for all my slow loss friends: no one knows what it's really like but us.

With much love,
Lois

BEFORE

THE PROM PARTY

1982

He knocks on the back door that leads into the kitchen. It's a humid, September Saturday night at my house two blocks from Narragansett Bay.

I don't like this plain, little two-bedroom ranch house. Last year, I moved from New York City to Rhode Island for a job and bought it. I thought the house would be a good investment, and I could swim in the bay all summer. It was a mistake.

The beach down the street is rocky, and the water isn't all that clean. Despite being by the water, I don't belong here with the families, lawnmowers, and suburbanites who are resigned to thinking that life is "always gonna be hard." They smoke on their front porches and tell me everything wrong with this small city.

I was too impulsive when I bought the house. My friends have warned me about being impulsive, especially when it comes to money and men. I make job choices based on how much money I can make, not bigger picture things like advancement opportunities or the work environment.

And guys? I fall for the handsome narcissists who are sexually thrilling and dead ends emotionally. I need to slow down and learn to make more considered choices.

But tonight, I'm not thinking about mistakes, my neighbors, or being cautious. Only about Handsome, a six-foot, thirty-four-year-old man with intelligent eyes, a runner's body, and a sensual voice that reeks of kindness and lust.

He walks into my kitchen dressed in a white dinner jacket with a rose on his lapel. He offers me a white box. Inside is a bouquet of pink and red flowers with streaming white satin ribbons. How did he know these would be the right colors to match my dress?

"Hey," he says. I put the box with the flowers on the orange laminate kitchen counter. He wraps me in his arms, teasing me with a kiss.

"What do you think?" I ask as I twirl around in my prom dress and show him all the decorations I've hung in the kitchen, which is almost as big as the rest of the two-bedroom ranch.

"Gorgeous. Just like you, Blue Eyes." I love it when he calls me Blue Eyes and sings the Elton John song of the same name.

The kitchen table and chairs are moved against the wall. Beer coolers sit under the bay window, which overlooks a sad patch of concrete pretending to be a patio.

There's another knock at the door. The DJs arrive with their massive speakers and other equipment.

I give Handsome a beer and lead the DJs down to the basement. It's a "finished" basement leftover from the sixties: brown paneling and wall-to-wall beige carpet. I've strung up "PROM" banners and strings of lights and put a disco ball on the ceiling.

THE PROM PARTY

The DJs test the system. The bass vibrates the house. My girl, Chaka Kahn, warms things up.

Chaka Khan
Chaka Khan

Chaka Khan, let me rock you
Let me rock you, Chaka Khan
Let me rock you, that's all I wanna do

The middle-aged neighbors on both sides have been asking about me, according to the kid who mows my lawn. This party should be a good introduction to who I am, responsible enough to buy a house at twenty-eight and still wild with life.

"Hey, you guys. Do you have the song "Wild Thing" by the Troggs? Can you play it at least twice? It's the theme song to my life."

Cars pull into the driveway and line the street on both sides. Friends arrive from Boston, New York, New Hampshire, and Providence. They have followed the invitation dress code: Wear what you wore to your high school prom. We are having a grown-up prom.

The guys wear powder blue tuxedos with matching paisley cummerbunds and bow ties. Only Handsome, eight years older than most of us, is classy in the white dinner jacket. The women's gowns are sparkly, low cut, and colorful. No boring black. They wear strapless, slinky dresses and floral gowns with puffed sleeves and cinched waists. Most, like me, are wearing their original prom dresses.

Why have we saved these dresses, especially after so many moves? Well, for a night like tonight, of course. We will dance all night. Sing. Act sloppy. Make out with our dates. Take corny prom pictures. Have much more fun than we ever had as insecure teenagers at our high school proms.

Two weeks before this prom I had gone to Block Island with a woman from work.

"About seven hundred guys are running the Run Around the Block 15k Road Race. Do you want to go with me?" asked Bev. "I've got a room reservation at the same hotel as some of my friends who will be running."

Bev also confessed that she had a thing for one of the guys running and didn't want to go alone. She didn't want to look like she was chasing him. I was game, especially if it involved seven hundred guys with skinny hips, strong legs, and short, clingy running shorts.

That's where I met Handsome, the guy Bev was chasing.

After the race, Bev, Handsome, and his friends and I danced at Dead Eye Dick's until 2:00 a.m. Here we were in our thirties and late twenties acting like rowdy teenagers. We laughed, sang, and drank bottles of beer as we walked back to the hotel. The Block Island boy cop stopped us at 3:00 a.m. for drinking and walking and gave us a warning citation.

The next morning, Bev wore an admirable chirpy Midwest attitude. She knew Handsome and I had some kind of wild magic going on.

On the ferry ride home on Sunday night, I told Handsome I was having a prom party. Did he want to be my date? He laughed at the silliness of the idea and said yes without hesitating.

The next night I called the guy who was supposed to be my prom date. "Geez, I'm sorry, Tom. I've had to cancel the prom."

"Do you want to come to Boston and hang out instead?" he asked.

"No, my sisters are going to come down," I lied. Bye, bye, Tom. I will do anything for this new man, my handsome prom date.

Eight weeks after the prom, we decide to go back to Block Island and get married.

THE PROM PARTY

Some people display pictures of their wedding day. For my husband and me, it's the prom party picture. I'm sitting on his lap in my pink floral prom dress, one arm wrapped around his neck, the other holding my bouquet, wearing what Bostonians would call a shit-eating grin.

FUDGE CAKE AND DEATH MARCHES

1988

We're celebrating in a tiny tea shop on the Isle of Skye. We eat chocolate fudge cake. It is moist and firm. Each piece of cake sits on a bone china dish covered in heavy cream.

I cut a small bite of cake and move it around the plate to soak up as much cream as possible. Then I quickly bring it up to my mouth, so I don't drop chocolate and cream over the one wool sweater I wear every day during this month-long vacation.

This is our fifth wedding anniversary. It is the first unrushed chunk of time we've had together. No wedding planning, house buying, job hunting, or any other commitments. We have time to wander, talk, and just be. No work deadlines. No expectations. No worries.

We sit around for days playing cribbage while waiting for the car ferry to the Orkney Islands. We get up at 3:00 a.m. to see the eclipse of the moon at an old Edwardian hunting lodge by the River Spey. We sleep in, make love, and miss the inn's breakfast. With a smirk, our New Zealand hosts tell us that they've left us a plate in the kitchen. They're off to forage mushrooms for dinner.

In another part of Scotland, we arrive at a grand estate not realizing this is where British aristocracy comes every year for the August holidays. There are no rooms available, says the very formal man at the reception desk, except for one in the back that's in the white, long-slung building where the help lives. We take the room, and he invites us to use the manor's drawing rooms but directs us to the local pubs for our meals. He cannot, unfortunately, accommodate us in the manor's dining room.

We love our squat, bare-bones room. We wash our clothes in the bathroom sink and string them up around the room to dry, turning the portable heater up to high. In the manor drawing room, we meet a couple about our age. Cambridge and Oxford, we learn. We play whist. They're surprised we know this card game. We play to win and do. My husband and I revel in the fact that we're such good card players together. We leave the aristocrats and return to the servants' quarters to put on our muddy boots and walk to the pub.

A surprise on this trip—and why we're celebrating in the tea shop—was a hike in Skye. We never took one another for granted after what happened.

"Be cautious now," we were warned. "Those mountains are like no other, and the weather is unpredictable."

We are unfazed. My husband is a mountain man. Hiking, skiing, rock climbing, ice climbing, running marathons up mountains. Mountains are his comfort place.

Halfway up a Skye mountain, we stop to drink some water. A strong gust blows a low cloud in from nowhere. We're blinded in the fog, and I feel the wind bend me forward. I am about to say something about it when my husband violently grabs my arm and yanks me toward him. He pulls me close, turns me around in his arms, and says, "Look."

As the cloud and wind move off, we stand silently and look out. Had he not grabbed me, I could have been blown into a three-thousand-foot ravine. I had been inches from the edge, unable to see in the dense fog of the cloud.

He kisses the top of my head, fearful, grateful.

We continue hiking. When we get to the top of the mountain, we eat our lunch and meet a local family doing the same. We tell them what had happened, and they nod and say it was no surprise.

"This isn't like the Alps," they say and tell us a few chilling hiking stories.

"Might we be able to hike down with you?" we ask. "This seems like a tricky one to navigate."

"That it is," they say and welcome us to join them.

We all pack up our lunch leftovers, rearrange the contents of our backpacks, and put on an extra rain layer. My husband offers a hand to help me up off my rock. When we turn to join the family, they are gone. They have disappeared into another massive, blinding cloud. We can't see or hear them. We yell to them. Nothing. Silence.

"Let's turn around and go down the way we came up," Greg says quietly and with no alarm or fear. His unflappability and perseverance increase my admiration for him. I feel fortunate to be married to someone so kind, logical, and grounded. I trust him with my whole being.

Back in the teahouse, I'm recovered enough to joke, though I'm done with Skye and its mountains.

SLOW LOSS

"You know I tease you that your 'little' hikes are like death marches," I say. "But *that*..."

"That was close," he says and gets up to get us another piece of fudge cake.

"With extra cream," I yell.

MORNING WALKS

2003

We are twenty years into marriage. An eight-year-old child. Demanding work. House maintenance. Sick parents. Vacations. Holiday parties. Dreams of what's next. And the morning walks, a sacred everyday ritual.

Greg and I catch up with one another on our walks.

We layer the clothes.

T-shirt. Fleece. Vest. Jacket. Hat. Gloves.

We shut the door and our Lab prances ahead, happy for another morning to explore. The sniffs are never the same.

Nor are we.

Some mornings we walk silently. A morning meditation without labeling it anything fancy or interesting. Just the one route or the other. Predictable. Comforting.

We pick up trash. Worry about the invasive vines smothering another tree. Step away to avoid the poison ivy. Disturb the heron who flees from the bush. Look down at the dew painting our boots.

SLOW LOSS

Some mornings we talk about the economy. Our businesses. Our family. House repairs. Politics. Feelings of uncertainty and unidentifiable malaise. We walk and talk.

A rhythm with no set beat.

Sometimes just an "mmm" to respond.

Sometimes letting the silence speak.

Sometimes the same points about the same topics, with more or less heat.

Always an unspoken contentment about starting the day together.

This ritual weaves a strong fabric into a long marriage.

This habit brings order to an unpredictable world.

This walking reassures us we're not alone. That even when we argue, we'll find our way back to one another. That even when the world feels overwhelming, we will walk and figure out a way forward.

MISSED SIGNS

2006

"How long do you think it will take this morning?" I ask my husband though I know the answer.

We're heading out of San Francisco on the 101 to Big Sur. We try to synch our business trips to San Francisco—mine in high-tech, his in the wine industry—so that we can take a few days off together and go to Big Sur. Sometimes we just go to Big Sur without business, usually in the winter. As others head for Disney World, our family heads for Big Sur. It's our place.

This morning I'm tired from last night's big meal.

"Those escargots were the best I've ever had," our eleven-year-old proclaims. He never had escargot before last night but loves all things exotic and dramatic.

"Just like his mother," my husband says.

I close my eyes to nap. We've driven this route so many times. There's nothing I'm going to miss.

When I wake, I'm disoriented. "Where are we, Greg?"

SLOW LOSS

"What do you mean? We're on our way to Big Sur."

I find a highway sign. We're on the 880 headed north to Oakland. We've driven in a big loop, almost to where we started but on the other side of the bay.

"We're going the wrong way. Get off at the next exit and turn around," I command. I stay alert for the rest of the ride. Pointing out when to exit.

"Let's stop at the beach before checking in," Greg says.

"Yeah, Mom, let's go to the beach," says Ian.

I'm upset and having a hard time reclaiming my free-spirit vacation attitude, but we park the car and go to the beach.

"Wow, Mom, look," our son says.

I think he's talking about this expansive beach with rock formations, so different from our flat, narrow New England beaches. Nope. What he sees is even more fascinating for the child who will eventually become a film artist. A movie is being shot on the beach.

He and his father walk to the shoot. I sit on a rock and watch them walk down the beach. I know something is wrong.

I list all the things I've tried to ignore. Greg's headaches, depression, tiredness, loss of interest in sex, reluctance to go to new places, and the vacant stare that sometimes comes over his face. And then today, getting lost on the simple drive to Big Sur that we've taken so many times.

Is this Alzheimer's? Greg's mother and her triplet brothers all disappeared from Alzheimer's by their midsixties, ending up in smelly nursing homes, staring vacantly, unable to form words or feed themselves. Greg is fifty-eight.

I see my little guy waving to me, urging me to walk down the beach to where the movie people are working.

But I cannot move.

MISSED SIGNS

I cannot run a business, raise a child, and lose my husband to Alzheimer's. What am I going to do? How is this going to play out? What should I do as soon as we get home?

The vacation is a disappointment. Aside from the first morning on the beach, it rained every day. We went to the movies and the Monterey Aquarium, played endless rounds of Trouble, watched movies in the hotel room, and ordered room service. All the things that we had never done before on our Big Sur trips. We are active, outside people. It all felt wrong. We should have stayed home.

"What do you think happened when we drove down here," I ask Greg. "Kind of weird that you got turned around. Do you think it might have anything to do with your headaches and the pinched nerve in your neck? Should we go to a specialist when we get home?"

"It was nothing. I was just tired."

DEATH AND DYING YEARS

2007–2009

We forgot about doctors and Greg's unusual health signs when we returned from Big Sur.

Greg's mother died in December 2007 from a long, slow loss to Alzheimer's. His father died six weeks later from congestive heart failure. My mother died three months after being diagnosed with small-cell lung cancer in 2009. My father had died in 2004. Life was a blur of nursing homes, hospice nurses, hospitals, funerals, and decisions about what to do with our parents' houses and belongings.

As Greg and I tried to manage family crises and run our businesses, we worried about Ian. He was emerging as a creative, metal-music-loving preteen with hair down to his waist and an obsession with playing online games like Minecraft and World of Warcraft. He did OK in school but never studied much. He had a few friends, also creative loners. Was his solitary nature normal for his age or a red flag? Would he be better at a small school?

"Don't worry," Greg assured me. "Ian and I have some deep talks when you're away on business. We cook together and talk about things that males don't want to discuss with their mothers. He's OK. But I'll spend more time with him and see if I can get him into running and track." (He did.)

One Saturday morning, I tried to catch up with Ian about what was happening in his world. How is school? How does he feel about so much death swirling around our lives? Is he looking forward to Merrowvista, the summer wilderness camp he loves?

"I'm good, Mom. School is fine. Don't worry about me. You know you worry and nag too much, don't you?"

I hug him, and he half reciprocates. He steps closer to me and puts his arms around me but doesn't let his hands touch my back for more than a millisecond.

"Mom, no more public displays of affection. I'm a teenager."

"Public displays? We're in our own kitchen."

"You know what I mean, Mom."

"Are you sure you're OK? You're not talking much."

"Mom. I'm fine. Really. Stop worrying so much."

Ian leaves to play a board game with friends. Greg is at work. The house is quiet.

I strip the sheets off our bed and then go into Ian's bedroom to do the same.

What a mess. It looks like a trash heap. School papers are strewn over his desk, and candy wrappers from the stash of Halloween candy Ian has hidden somewhere are on the floor. There are unused three-ring binders, pencils that need to be sharpened, and scraps of paper with passwords and email addresses scribbled on them.

DEATH AND DYING YEARS

I look through the papers on the desk and find poems written for English class. They are dark and all about death. Ian seems so sweet, positive, and funny, but these poems are upsetting.

I read the last one and realized he has been internalizing his grandparents' deaths. Though I'm calmly panicked, I see that this teenager, so reluctant to display affection, was torn up about his grandmother's recent death.

FORGET TO REMEMBER

Every morning,
Not knowing if she will wake up.
Day by day, she's getting pulled away.
Farther and farther into darkness.
Denial is the only thing that can comfort her.
Right after anger, acceptance,
And Death.
If only there was a way
To forget to remember
This is not happening.

During these turbulent years, I am so grateful that Ian and Greg's bond deepened. Watching them together, I see how much they admire, trust, and love one another.

I nag and worry. Greg listens and encourages.

After the parental death and dying years, we slid back to normality, enjoying the absence of family crises and the everyday pleasures of dinners together, Ian's art progress, walking the dog, seeing friends, and planning a summer vacation.

Greg's primary care physician suggested monthly B12 shots to see if they might help. We kept our fingers crossed that this B12 deficiency could be the underlying cause of Greg's mysterious symptoms.

Then, we forgot about the weird ailments again. A secret from Greg's past changed our priorities.

FAMILY CHANGES: THE LOST SON

2010

It was the day after Christmas, and I had to do something. Our dog's suffering and had gone on far too long. The coughing, the gasping for air, the inability to eat.

"We have to put Ace down. Today, if we can get into the vet," I said in my don't-mess-with-me-on-this tone.

Greg gave me the same sad, big-eyed, loving look as our dying black Lab, whose official name was Acela "Ace" Midnight. Our only child, Ian, was four years old when we got Ace, and he had been in charge of selecting the puppy from the litter and naming it. At that age, Ian had been obsessed with riding trains, especially the new ultramodern Acela. The puppy was so black that Ian had insisted that Midnight also be part of his name.

But during this week after Christmas, we three would have to help our gentle, steady Ace out of the suffering that had been getting progressively worse since the summer.

"It seems like everyone I love is dead or dying," Greg said as I pushed him to call the animal hospital. Grief had hung like mistletoe in our lives this Christmas. My mother, our beloved family matriarch, had died six months earlier, and Greg's parents had died the year before, just six weeks apart from each other. Our Christmas rituals were in flux; we were middle-aged orphans trying to figure out how to create our own traditions.

The next morning, Greg and Ian lifted Ace into the truck. It had been months since the dog could hop in there himself.

Ironically, Ace seemed better that morning. He wasn't coughing, his tail was doing its happy morning wag, and his eyes were clear. None of that filmy gunk was crusted in their creases.

"Maybe it's not time," Greg and Ian said to me, knowing in their hearts that it was.

The vet gave Ace a shot to relax him, and then we spent fifteen minutes crying, rubbing his belly, and assuring him not to worry. Before giving him the final shot, the vet told us that Ace had a large mass near his intestines, so we were doing the right thing. We left with his collar and tags, returning home for the rest of the Christmas vacation.

During our annual neighborhood New Year's Eve party a few days later, the talk was centered on dogs.

"I think I'm going to take a rest from dogs for a while," Greg told some friends early in the evening. This was code for "I can't bear having my heart broken anymore."

Yet as soon as our guests left, Greg was online, engrossed in a New Hampshire breeder's website that a neighbor had recommended

FAMILY CHANGES: THE LOST SON

during the party. By noon of New Year's Day, he had talked to the breeder, reserved a puppy from a soon-to-be litter, and scheduled a day later to go to New Hampshire to meet the next member of our family.

For the next two days, Greg kept beckoning Ian and me over to his computer to look at the breeder's dogs. He was especially excited that our puppy would be a half-sister to Maggie, a Lab owned by one of our friends. That he had decided on a female chocolate Lab rather than a male black Lab like Ace was more reason to "Come, look at this."

I had had enough of looking at puppy photos. I just wanted to sit quietly and read a book.

The next day, the last day of Christmas vacation, Greg called me over again. "You might want to come and see this email," he said.

"Later," I said.

"No," he said quietly, with a weird blank expression. "Come see."

The Facebook message was from his son: the son he hadn't seen in thirty-seven years; the son he had allowed his ex-wife's second husband to adopt; the son who was Gregory John Junior but now had a Jewish last name instead of his original Portuguese one.

Two months earlier, Greg had learned his son's name and where he worked: he was a veterinarian at a Miami animal hospital. He started following the animal hospital's Facebook page and "liked" and commented on several posts.

His son was writing to say he knew who he was. He was reaching out across a messy history, not of his making, but full of twisted assumptions, fears, regrets, self-deceptions, lies, manipulations, and longings for love lost.

For the next several weeks, Greg and Greg Jr. lobbed emails back and forth—forehands, backhands, soft lobs, steady volleys—asking, explaining, confessing, testing, and unsure what to do next.

SLOW LOSS

"Just get on a plane and go to him," I urged in my don't-mess-with-me-on-this tone. But these men needed their logical, left-brained selves to cover safe, factual territory before they could meet. Emailing each other provided emotional cover for deep wounds.

As one blizzard after another slammed us that January, the emails kindled forgiveness and love. We woke every morning hoping that there would be a new email from Greg Jr.

Throughout our long marriage, Greg kept a photo of this first son on his bedroom bureau. He was a blond eighteen-month-old sitting on a swing, his hands tightly holding the chains, his eyes squinting in the sun, and his blue shorts and white shirt with the Peter Pan collar looking uncomfortable. Many mornings, I picked up that fading photograph and wondered about this lost child.

One Sunday night, when we first started dating, Greg told me there was something I needed to know about him, and once I knew, he would understand if I didn't want to see him anymore.

My mind went wild. Did he have a criminal record? AIDS? Psychosis?

"I have a son who I let be adopted," he said softly. "I thought he'd have a better, more stable life with his mother and her new husband. I was a mess after the divorce, sleeping around and hanging out with some weird characters before I finally moved back to Rhode Island from Miami. I hope I did the right thing. Some people think what I did is horrible. I usually don't tell people because I know how they'll react."

I moved close to him, and we held each other a long time. How could I judge a man with so much hurt and such pure intentions?

Now, as Greg packed to go to Miami to meet his newfound son, daughter-in-law, and granddaughter, our dinner conversations included an important and enjoyable topic.

FAMILY CHANGES: THE LOST SON

"What should Kelsey call me?" Greg wondered.

Ian and I came up with all sorts of possibilities, having as much fun suggesting grandfather monikers as Ian had had when he named Ace.

"Grandfather, like in *Heidi*," I said.

"Vovô, for Portuguese grandfather," said Ian.

When Greg walked through the Miami airport and saw his newfound family, he stopped for a moment and then had a hard time moving. Though he hadn't yet been diagnosed, the anxiety of meeting his son triggered classic Parkinson's symptoms. His body stiffened, making it hard to move. In this "freeze," he couldn't move his feet.

Then seven-year-old Kelsey ran to the grandfather she had never known and put her arms around him, saying, "Grandpa!" With this new granddaughter's joy, his body relaxed, and he was able to move and meet his son, Greg Jr.

I would like to tell you this story has a happy ending.

Because it does.

"I never wanted to find you," Greg Jr. said when he met his father after all those years. "I thought you'd be an asshole like my mother's other husbands. I can understand why you left her, but how could you have left me with her?"

Some questions can never be answered.

Another miracle of this story is that my stepson was not bitter and held no grudges, and that forgiveness was knitted into his soul. How could he be so like the father who didn't raise him?

We also got the new chocolate Lab that winter. Greg named the puppy this time, calling her Maia after the goddess of spring, the time of year when new life and growth burst open in uncontrollable ways.

Greg's odd body aches, nightmares, and tiredness continued, but in our joy, we ignored them.

DURING: THE EARLY YEARS

COMING OUT AS A FRAUD

2011

Two hundred people are about to enter the ballroom. They don't know this will be my coming-out party as a fraud. Neither do I.

It's another bland hotel ballroom set up for a conference: no windows, beige carpeting, tan wallpaper, brown chairs around tables for eight. A screen and projector are set up in the front. I plug my PC into the projector, strap the lavalier pack onto the waist of my pants, and attach the mic to my blazer. Check, check, check. As a professional speaker, I've gone through this setup for more than twenty years.

I look good, even with the bulge of the lavalier pack under my blazer. The reds and fuchsias of my sweater blazer set me apart from the ballroom bland. It's my speaker's uniform.

I am here to speak about the book I wrote about helping my mother die from cancer, *Be the Noodle: 50 Ways to Be a Courageous, Compassionate, Crazy-Good Caregiver.*

SLOW LOSS

I know conference audiences want to be entertained and learn one or two useful things. Whether I'm talking about digital marketing, organizational change, or helping my mother die, I know people want to leave with warm and fuzzy, can-do feelings. They want a little bit of inspiration and confidence that they, too, can do this.

The organizer tells me that the two hundred hospice nurses, CNAs, and families of hospice patients will begin to file into the room at 1:15. She'll introduce me at 1:30, and then I'll have an hour to talk and take questions.

"They're going to love your ideas on how to care for someone who's dying," she assures me. "You're so positive and pragmatic."

It is 2011, two years after my mother died, one year after publishing a book on how to be a "courageous, compassionate, crazy-good caregiver," and six months since the International Hospice Association gave it a book-of-the-year endorsement.

It is one day since my husband was diagnosed with Parkinson's disease. He is sixty-three. I am fifty-five.

We had been going from specialist to specialist since 2005, trying to figure out why he was dizzy, had relentless headaches, had a couple of weird falls, and screamed in his sleep. Migraines? Pinched nerve? Depression? MS? Stress from the 2008 financial crash and running a wine shop? Anxiety from raising a teenager and recently reuniting with the child he allowed to be adopted forty years ago?

"Has he ever hurt you at night?" the new neurologist asked yesterday.

We looked at each other. Should we tell? We've told no one about what's gone on at night. It's so bizarre and intimate in a violent sort of way.

"He hits me when he's having nightmares," I told him. "Two weeks ago, he tried to strangle me. We can't sleep in the same bed. I'm too scared."

The neurologist turned to Greg for acknowledgment. Greg nodded, embarrassed. He can have a temper when people try to control him or tell him what he should or shouldn't do, like his late father and several of his bosses when he worked in the corporate world. At his core, Greg is kind and thoughtful. He has never hit me or our teenage son. This new nighttime dream demon is unpredictable, angry, mean, and loud. Who is this weird nocturnal creature inhabiting Greg's body? Is it trying to warn us: "Beware, danger lies ahead"?

"Based on your other symptoms and the REM behaviors, I am 99 percent sure that you have Parkinson's disease," said the neurologist. "It's a slow-moving disease, and you are likely to have many good years living with it. I like to think of it as more of a disorder than a disease. You are just sixty-three years old and are likely to live a long life."

How am I going to do this talk? How can I be confident, knowledgeable, and entertaining when I feel like I'm falling into a void with no one to catch me? How can I offer useful tips when my mother died within three months of her cancer diagnosis? It's easy to sprint and care for someone for three months or even a year. You can see a finish line in three months or a year. I am a sprinter. Short books, intense but small-scale client projects, home renovations that last a Saturday afternoon, and long walks but no steep hikes. I like to finish fast. This Parkinson's thing could be years and years of slow and steady decline. A marathon.

Greg is the marathoner. Not me.

How do I live with and care for a person with a disorder? What does it mean to be a disordered person? In addition to being a sprinter, I am orderly. I like predictability, YouTube how-to videos, a clean, neat house, and the comfort of knowing how to work with an audience. I am a Firestarter, a sprinkler of magic, positivity, fairy dust, and a fixer of easy things.

Am I overreacting? The neurologist said Greg could live a long time. He's always been super healthy.

I cannot do this talk today. I am a fraud. I don't know anything. I'm out of gas. Please, God, get me out of here. Why didn't I cancel yesterday after we got the news? Why did I go back to work the day after I had a miscarriage sixteen years ago? Why did I move in with my mother to help her die without thinking about what my fourteen-year-old son was going through in middle school? Why do I accept lucrative business gigs when I feel overextended? Why am I so dutiful? Why can't I take a day off? Why can't I just power through this as I usually do when feeling anxious? Why can't I stop?

I hear my recently dead mother speaking in my head: "You can do this." I want to be like my mother—resourceful, action-oriented, calm amid chaos, and masterful in tamping down her emotions. The ultimate "stay calm and carry on" woman. Usually, I'm quite good at being like this too. Why is this meltdown happening today? Greg is not dying. He just has Parkinson's. Get a grip, girl.

The ballroom doors open, and people stream in and take seats. I go from table to table, introduce myself, and ask people what attracted them to this talk.

"I'm a CNA with Bay State Health, and I like how you make hospice sound less scary for people."

"I lost my mother, too, and I wish I had known more of your tips when I was caring for her."

"My husband has colon cancer."

"I'm a palliative care nurse."

The organizer taps on the mic. I join her in the front of the room. She finishes the introduction, people applaud, and I freeze. I can't give any advice, be charming, or instill optimism, or call up a can-do spirit.

The talk is a bomb.

The only thing I can do is tell people the truth. "I'm sorry. I'm a mess. Yesterday, I found out my husband has Parkinson's disease. I don't know how I'm going to do this."

I stumbled through some slides and ideas about how to care for someone who is dying.

After it's over, a few people share stories of people they know who have Parkinson's and remind me of how well Michael J. Fox is doing, how well their brother is doing after deep-brain stimulation to manage his Parkinson's, how well their friend's next door neighbor is doing since his diagnosis.

I want to believe them.

MR. PERSEVERANCE'S FIRST TOUR OF DUTY

2013

"Greg, what are your results? What are your top strengths?"

"Perseverance, kindness, perspective, honesty, and love of beauty and excellence."

"Oh, those definitely sound like you. Especially perseverance and kindness."

"What are yours?"

"Honesty, bravery, creativity, and love of beauty and excellence."

We high-five one another.

We agree that we have a perfect combination of strengths to handle any situation that might be thrown at us.

Greg and I are at a four-day Parkinson's wellness program at the Kripalu Center for Yoga and Health, a former Jesuit monastery set on one hundred acres of beautiful grounds in western Massachusetts.

SLOW LOSS

The program, sponsored by The Parkinson's Foundation, features lectures by neurologists, nutritionists, and therapists specializing in resiliency. There is yoga, meditation, journey dancing, journaling, and support group sessions for people with PD and their caregivers. It's billed as a Western-Eastern medicine approach, physical health and spiritual health, body and mind, resiliency and relaxation.

Greg's favorite sessions are meditation and participation in a support group every afternoon for people who have been diagnosed with PD for five years or less. All the PD participants are men, and they display few symptoms. Most are still skiing, hiking, traveling, and living a pretty good life. These discussions boost Greg's optimism. The disease no longer feels ominous.

I also like my breakout group. It is for partners of people with PD. The two predominant themes are how to handle spouses' denials of their disease symptoms and how to live without worrying about what might happen as the disease progresses. Most of us are women. We agree that we are world-class worriers. The therapist reminds us that worrying helps no one, nor will it alter what happens.

"Did worrying about whether your teenager would get home safe actually help him or her get home?"

We laugh. So true.

My other favorite session is the yoga nidra, which may be the most relaxing thing I've ever learned how to do. You lie on a mat, listen to New Age music, and kind facilitators tuck a blanket around you, rub your head, and reassure you it's OK to fall asleep.

Greg and I find the session on identifying and using innate strengths fascinating and practical. Aside from the exuberant free-form dancing every day at lunch, this is our favorite session.

Psychologist Maria Sirois, author of *A Short Course in Happiness and Loss: (And Other Dark, Difficult Times)*, explains that the field

MR. PERSEVERANCE'S FIRST TOUR OF DUTY

of positive psychology has identified twenty-four universal character traits that all of us have, some much stronger than others. When we use our top three to five "signature" strengths, we can decrease stress and increase our well-being.

Maria tells us that when we understand our spouse's strengths, we can appreciate one another in new ways—and help one another get through difficult periods by remembering to lean on our strengths.

"How can we apply the knowledge of our strengths? Here's how," she explains.

"A difficult moment comes. Perhaps a diagnosis like PD. Perhaps the loss of a job. Perhaps a new opportunity that requires great change. You center yourself and take out your list. Choose one of your strengths. Just one. You apply that strength to your daily life for the next week, even if you only do it for a moment.

"An example from my own life: One of my core strengths is compassion. When our income suddenly became severely reduced a few years ago, the bills began to pile and tension in our home mounted. I took out my list, chose one of my gifts—compassion—and spent the next seven days practicing it.

"One day, I called a former colleague who had lost her mother and just listened to her grieve. The next day, I wrote a note to my teenage daughter, who I knew was deeply worried. The third day, I visited a local shelter and offered my help. The fourth day, I let a mom with screaming children go ahead of me in line at the supermarket. The fifth day, I spent ten minutes meditating on self-compassion. The sixth day, I wrote a note to a woman I had read about in our local paper who had just lost an infant son. The seventh day, I took time in the morning to review my acts of compassion and see what had happened.

"What did I notice? I had more energy, calmness, and clarity about what needed to be done next to help our family get through our crisis.

"What had changed externally? Nothing. We were still in difficult straits. What had changed internally? Everything. I had reminded myself of who I was and what I had to bring to the world—no matter what the world was bringing to me. I remembered that I had more than one strength to bear, and I had taken charge of the one thing I actually had control over myself in the present moment.

"As you deal with the many years of PD, lean on your strengths. Resilience is not something you have, or you don't have. Our actions and behaviors build our capacity to be resilient."

When we got home that weekend, I emailed Maria to thank her for the program and told her how it helped us reclaim positivity in our lives. This was a big shift from how we felt when Greg was diagnosed with PD two years ago.

Greg and I felt elated and connected as a couple. We were not going to let this disease diagnosis drag us into a mindset of doom and worry.

Plus it was June, the most glorious time of year in New England. Greg had recently sold his small wine shop and was relieved. No more weekends at work, managing staff, worrying about cash flow, driving into the city in the middle of the night when the store alarm goes off.

Greg Jr. was opening an animal hospital in Miami, and Greg was helping him with finance and other small business issues. Greg reassured his son that despite frustrations with banks and real estate build-out issues, the hospital would be a success. Mr. Perseverance-Kindness would not let his son's dream derail.

MR. PERSEVERANCE'S FIRST TOUR OF DUTY

Tomorrow night, Ian will graduate from high school, drive up to New Hampshire the next day for a summer job at a camp, and then go to art school in Savannah in the fall.

Life is good.

Ian has left for graduation ceremony preparations. I'm getting dressed. Greg is outside talking to our new neighbor, Marna. Her chocolate lab, Bunny, and our chocolate lab, Maia, are the same age and temperament. They are three years old but are mischievous, wild, strong, and still not obeying commands.

I hear a dog shriek and Greg yell.

I run outside. "What happened?"

"Maia and Bunny were chasing each other, and Maia barreled into Greg's leg," said Marna. "I think I heard a crack."

"Greg, should I take you to the ER?"

"No. It's Ian's graduation. I can't miss that. Put Maia in her kennel, and let's go. I'll be fine."

Greg was not fine. Despite the pain, he walked into the auditorium and sat for an hour waiting to see Ian cross the stage and receive his diploma. As soon as Ian left the stage, Greg said, "I need to get to a hospital."

A fire marshal helped Greg out of the building and into my car.

The emergency room was jammed. We waited three hours before a doctor ordered X-rays and examined Greg's leg.

"You have a fracture in your lower leg," said the attending physician. "There's nothing we can do tonight. Go home, call an orthopedic surgeon in the morning, and get an appointment. We'll give names of some orthopedic surgeons and send a pain medication prescription to the CVS all-night pharmacy."

We got home at 2:00 a.m.

"This is more than a broken leg. The pain is like nothing I've ever experienced," said Greg. We were up all night. Greg's pain was acute. The pain medication provided no relief.

At 6:00 a.m. I called Greg's brother.

"Isn't your neighbor Mike an orthopedic surgeon? Can you call him to see how quickly Greg could get in to see him this morning?"

The surgeon/neighbor told me to call his office at 9:00 a.m. When I called, the receptionist said the doctor could fit Greg in at 2:00 p.m., twenty-two hours since the dog ran into Greg's leg.

"I think this may be more than a broken leg," Dr. Mike said after examining the leg. He asked another surgeon to come in and take a look at Greg. They inserted a needle into Greg's lower leg to measure the pressure in his muscles near the fracture.

"Did the hospital do a compartment syndrome test," the doctors asked.

"No, just an X-ray."

"Greg, you have acute Compartment Syndrome. Your muscle and nerve tissue have been cut off from their blood supply. We need to do emergency surgery this afternoon to alleviate the pressure. Without oxygen and nutrients, your muscles and nerves may stop functioning or die. If the hospital had done a simple pressure test last night, you wouldn't be in this situation. I would have thought that was standard procedure at the ER."

Greg's first surgery was three hours later. There had already been tissue death (necrosis) and likely long-term damage to his leg.

Over the next ten days, Greg had two more fasciotomy surgeries to remove additional muscle in his leg to create space and relieve the

MR. PERSEVERANCE'S FIRST TOUR OF DUTY

pressure. At one point, cardiologists get involved. They were concerned that the muscle tissue in his heart was also affected.

Greg left the hospital after two weeks. At home, his leg is connected to a 24/7 wound drainage machine for several weeks to drain the fluid and prevent infection. He still has the fracture, but that surgery can't be done until the gaping wounds in his leg heal, which will be at least eight weeks. He will have permanent foot drop, impairing his mobility. His heart needs to be monitored. Like PD wasn't enough.

"We're going to get through this," says Mr. Perseverance.

And we do.

Greg lifts weights in the hospital bed we've put in the downstairs den.

"The stronger my upper body is, the more I'll be able to compensate for my leg," he says.

He asks the visiting nurses how he might be able to rewrap his leg bandages every day without my help. (Not possible.) He researches experimental Botox treatments that may help improve his dropped foot. (Not effective) He calls a contractor to install grab bars in the bathroom. (So helpful.) He pressures the surgeon to do the leg fracture surgery as soon as possible because he needs to be on a plane to Savannah in early September to take Ian to college. (Say, what?)

"You are not going to Savannah," I said, calling up all my bravery and honesty strengths. "You can hardly walk. Ian will understand, Greg."

"We can do this. Please find an inn with a room on the first floor and a handicapped bathroom. This is important to me. My father didn't take me to college. I was on my own. I don't want Ian to feel like I did. I want to be better to my sons than my father was to me."

I admire Greg's tenacity and his tender love for his sons. But I worry about taking a trip after everything that has happened this summer. I can take Ian to SCAD and get him settled into his dorm. It's no big deal.

But off we went.

Even using wheelchairs and porters, the travel exhausted Greg. While Ian and I spent two days buying sheets, towels, lamps, and other dorm necessities, Greg sat on the porch of our inn.

Our room and one other room at the inn were handicapped accessible.

"Once a month, I invite a disabled vet and his wife or girlfriend for a free weekend at the inn," explained the inn owner. "It's tragic what these young kids have been through in Iraq and Afghanistan. They've been blown to pieces, burned, and scarred emotionally. A nice young guy and his fiancée are in the room across from yours."

When Ian and I return to the inn to pick Greg up for dinner, we find him talking with a former Army Ranger whose legs have been amputated.

"I told Sam about when I was stationed here at Hunter during Vietnam. Sam fought the Taliban in Afghanistan," Greg says.

Greg spent the next day talking to Sam as well. On our flight home, he sat next to another veteran whose arm and leg had been amputated.

"These guys are so positive. They are young, making plans for the future, and are not bitter or angry about what's been taken from them. I have nothing to complain about. I am sixty-five and have lived most of my life with a healthy body. I am so fortunate."

Greg will mention these inspiring men for the rest of his life. Like him, their dominant strengths are perseverance and perspective.

THE PLOT CHANGES

2014–2018

Aside from losing leg muscle and learning to walk with a dropped foot, Greg's next four years living with Parkinson's were uneventful. Not great, but OK. Believe the experts when they say you can live many good years with the disease.

Changes were gradual.

Some foods became harder to swallow. Greg gave up driving and started using a rollator to walk more securely. Our morning walks shrank from a couple of miles to half a mile, to a few houses up and back, to "Why don't you go on a walk without me."

The disease was slow-moving, and we tried to match that pace.

Then, the disease moved faster and more unpredictably, especially the cognitive and behavioral changes.

When something unexpected happens in our family, our response is, "Plot change!" It reminds us life is unpredictable and we need to adapt.

Eight years into Greg's disease, the plot changed.

SLOW LOSS

No doctors prepared us for it. Few disease associations tell you about how damn hard and unpredictable it is.

The following is what happened during the last four years of Greg's twelve-year PD journey.

DURING: 2019

THE VOICE

When I'm away for a night, I call Greg to check in and make sure he hasn't fallen or choked on food. Not that he'd tell me. He likes to protect me from what's happening.

"Maybe I shouldn't go away this weekend with my sisters. What if you fell?"

"I am fine. You worry too much, and I'm not as bad as you think. I always manage to get myself up after a fall, and I've never hurt myself. Stop the nagging. If something happens, I'll call one of the neighbors."

It is year nine since his diagnosis.

So, I go to Cape Cod, Maine, or Boston for an occasional weekend—away but not more than a two-hour drive from home.

I call home and hear his calm, deep voice—the same voice that first called me all those years ago on the wall phone in my kitchen, where we had the prom party. His voice is soothing and slow. He listens and responds thoughtfully, not fast and reactive like me.

This beautiful voice, still.

When we're together, and I see the effects of Parkinson's, I can't hear him. Fear makes me deaf.

SLOW LOSS

The dyskinesia makes him rock back and forth, from one foot to the other. Or he taps on the dining table with his right hand for hours, wearing away the paint. Eating is becoming an issue. If Greg eats too quickly or eats difficult-to-chew foods like beef, he has trouble swallowing the food. He has mastered the ability to stick his fingers in his throat to trigger a gag reflux.

We sit down for dinner every night as we've done throughout our marriage. Now, he usually gets up from the table halfway through the meal and goes to the bathroom. I clear the table and listen to him vomit.

But when I call him on the phone, I only hear his voice. Not the decline.

It is the same voice that seduced me all those years ago at the prom. The same sensual voice that calmly said, "Let's keep going," after he grabbed me just before a wind gust almost pushed me off a Skye mountain. The voice that is steady, reassuring, and kind.

Even during our most memorable fights, the voice was even, level, and deep. He would slam doors, but the voice never wavered.

The night we discovered that our teenage son had snuck out to a dangerous club in Providence, Greg called him. No yelling, just calmly telling Ian to leave the club, walk to Greg's store, and wait there until he could pick him up. The voice was calm and firm.

Speaking softly or in a slurred, mumbling way is a common symptom of Parkinson's.

So far, we are spared.

Oh, his voice.

SOMETIMES WHEN LISTENING

Sometimes, we forget about the disease.

Sometimes, we hear a great horned owl outside the bedroom window.

Sometimes, I go out the next morning to the bush that brushes up against the window to find a trace of the owl. There are no traces. It's hard to imagine that an owl could perch on this scrawny shrub.

Sometimes, I hear what I need to hear. Sometimes, I don't hear my husband.

Sometimes, I try to control too much, which makes him crazy.

Sometimes, I open everything too fast. My mouth, my heart, and the bedroom window when I hear my owl. My speed scares the owls and my husband. He is slow and deliberate. I am fast.

Sometimes, when I try to go more slowly, I get bored, shop for stuff I don't need, daydream about going to Big Sur, and criticize my competencies as a wife, mother, and neighbor. I retreat into work, where I am rewarded for being fast.

SLOW LOSS

Sometimes, when I try to go slowly, I see the tracks in the virgin winter snow. Fox or coyote? I follow the tracks, looking for scat. As I get deeper into the woods, I remember my friends who have moved on from our woods to true wilderness. They go into the forest after midnight to search for a snowy owl. They rarely find it, but the fun is the possibility, knowing you might hear the owl's purr if you're quiet and still.

Sometimes, I slow my consulting business down to be with Greg and our family more.

Sometimes, slowing down makes me want to go faster. I love the surprises, the frustrations, and the rush of corporate life. The travel to unknown cities. The anticipation of not knowing what will happen with a new group of clients. The anxiety around wondering whether the combination of people and ideas will ignite into something powerful. The inability to sleep because of the energy and magic we created together.

Sometimes, my mind slows me down and questions my relevance. That was then. The now is different. That life is gone. It's another loss. Let it go.

But who am I? If I slow life down, can I still grow or will I shrink?

Sometimes, I should listen more to the owl than my mind. The owl, a symbol of wisdom and guidance, is quiet and consistent, perceptive and purposeful. The owl reminds me to slow down and appreciate the present.

Sometimes, the promise of hearing the owl is enough to keep listening and walking in the woods on a frigid night. Sometimes, the promise of sitting together on the back deck and spotting a bald eagle is enough to keep zigzagging in a long marriage. How is it possible that we've been married for thirty-two years?

Sometimes, when I stop trying to hear what I think I want or need, I am surprised by life.

SOMETIMES WHEN LISTENING

It's the owl outside my window. It's Greg cheerfully greeting me in the morning and telling me I look beautiful. It's a dream where my dead mother tells me not to worry so much and assures me I'm doing my best.

It is not what I expected to hear. And it is magnificent.

OUT-OF-CONTROL IMPULSE CONTROL

Greg saw his neurologist once a year at the beginning of this disease. Then, it was twice a year. After nine years, he saw the neurologist every three to four months.

For all these years, the neurologist has always welcomed Greg into his office with a handshake and friendly, "And how are you doing, Mr. Matta?"

Not today. He knows by looking at my husband. The dyskinetic arms, head, and legs sway like each limb is dancing to a different beat of music. Greg drops his wallet, has trouble getting out of his jacket, and fidgets with his phone.

"You're going to have to put that away for now," Dr. Friedman says like a kind, no-nonsense parent. No phones at the neurologist's office.

The conversation is difficult today. Greg's disease has worsened a lot in the last six months. We list the new challenges: falls, compulsive buying, an escalating porn addiction, difficulty swallowing, more frequent hallucinations, and increasing incontinence.

The doctor explains that these are common behaviors associated with advanced PD, suggests some medication changes, and asks if there are any other concerns.

"Yes," says Greg with sudden clarity and confidence. "I think my wife should have an affair. I don't care if she sees someone else. She's the one making me worse. I would be better without her."

"Do you think she's having an affair now?" asks the doctor. "It's very common for men with Parkinson's to accuse their wives of having affairs. It's part of the paranoia."

"No, I don't think she is. But she should. I don't care. She should find some guy to sleep with."

I should be used to my husband's unfiltered comments by now, but they always catch me by surprise and rattle me.

When good friends visit, Greg's social filters fall away, and he blurts out whatever pops into his mind. When he gets excited, his rational brain seems to shut off.

"Do you know you have big hairs growing on your chin?" Greg asked one of my friends when she came for dinner. Like menopause isn't bad enough.

"Hey, look who it is. It's the Pillsbury Doughboy. You have gotten SO fat," Greg said to a friend we hadn't seen in a few years.

"Gee, thanks Greg, good to see you, too."

I take friends aside, apologize, and tell them it's the disease. They laugh and say they understand. I am so lucky to have friends who understand what this disease is doing to Greg and show up even when I lie and say, "I'm fine."

The most difficult things to hear are Greg's continued accusations that I am the cause of his disease symptoms.

"She makes me paranoid and anxious," he repeatedly tells his primary care physician and friends. "I am fine. She's the one making me like this."

OUT-OF-CONTROL IMPULSE CONTROL

As Dr. Friedman starts wrapping up this visit, he asks me if there has been any other unusual behavior.

"Yes, Greg bought a new car online without telling me."

"Is this true, Mr. Matta?"

"Yes, I wanted a car, so I bought one. It's my money, I can do what I want. She can't stop me."

Greg has not driven in five years. He is still cognitively astute enough to figure out how to buy a car online without having to go to an auto dealership.

Two friends from my Parkinson's support group have had similar experiences with their husbands making big purchases without telling them. One husband bought a $60,000 car that he's never been able to drive, and another bought a yacht.

When you have Parkinson's, nerve cells (neurons) in the substantia nigra part of the brain die. Without these neurons, the brain stops producing dopamine, a neurotransmitter that regulates movement and cognitive functions like memory, mood, concentration, and the brain's pleasure pathways. Most PD patients eventually take a drug called carbidopa-levodopa, which mimics the effects of dopamine and allows them to function physically and cognitively.

But carbidopa-levodopa doesn't always help with impulse control dysfunction, like buying a car online.

Greg also buys in quantities of ten or twenty, whether it is cereal, toilet paper, lightbulbs, flashlights, or porn subscriptions.

Financially, his patterns are less predictable. He has opened thirty-eight CD accounts and twelve credit cards.

This is a man who had been deliberate and rational in making decisions. Where I could be impulsive, he slowed down and thought things through. Now, his behavior feels wild and reckless.

SLOW LOSS

At the end of the visit, the neurologist increases the dose of Greg's carbidopa-levodopa to try to better manage escalating behavioral and physical changes.

Nothing stops his impulsive buying and behavior.

DURING: 2020

EVIL HOUSE SPIRITS

I don't want to tell you about the house on a small pond where we lived for thirty-six years because it is too painful.

Our house was the perfect home. It was a huge step up from my little ranch house where we had the prom party. From the front, it looked like a traditional Cape Cod-style house, but the back looked modern, with big windows overlooking the pond.

The house had open and cozy spaces, a Scandinavian wood stove in the sunroom, a gas fireplace in the living room, mahogany walls, and built-in bookcases in the den. My office space over the garage had a 9 ft. x 6 ft. custom window looking out to the pond. The kitchen also had giant windows, soapstone counters, and open dining and living room views.

A large wall of French doors from the dining room opened out to a deck. An expansive German-made awning covered the deck in the summer, creating a little waterfront oasis.

When we bought the house, it was a mess. Every year we'd save money and do a project. Pull up wall-to-wall carpeting and sand the oak floors underneath. Rip down frumpy wallpaper and paint the walls in soothing green and blue shades. Turn a screened-in porch into an all-year sunroom. Tear down walls. Install bigger windows. Paint the exterior. Throw out our hand-me-down furniture and buy a twelve-foot-long French country farm table or a four-poster antique bed. Toss framed posters from our thirties and replace them with original art from local artists.

Every December, we helped our neighbors put up a Christmas tree in the middle of the pond. Its lights sparkled on the darkest winter nights.

And the parties. Our house was the gathering spot for family and friends on Christmas, Thanksgiving, New Year's, Fourth of July, birthdays, office parties, and any other reason to celebrate.

There was only one problem with the house. Well, two. The bedrooms and full bath were upstairs. We turned the downstairs den into a bedroom for Greg. The bathroom was more problematic.

We installed railings on both sides of the stairs to give Greg more support. We laid carpeting on the once-bare oak steps so he'd have some traction and wouldn't slip. (Meanwhile, we removed all the rugs in the house so he wouldn't trip on them.) We also installed grab bars and a seat in the shower, which, unfortunately, was not a walk-in shower.

Shower days were becoming exhausting for Greg. Some weeks he wanted to avoid it all altogether.

I looked into a chair lift, but the design of our stairway made that problematic. There was also no room to expand the half-bath downstairs into a full bath.

"Marna is thinking of selling her house. We should buy it. It's all on one level and has walk-in showers. And we'd still be living on the pond," I suggested.

EVIL HOUSE SPIRITS

"The only way you'll ever get me out of this house is in a box. End of story."

Our neighbor, Marna, lived two houses down from us. Ten years before, she bought a small ranch house, gutted it, expanded the foundation, and built a modern beauty, also with floor-to-ceiling windows overlooking the pond.

I was always a bit suspicious of the house. Marna slipped on the ice while getting out of her car at 11:00 p.m. on a frigid January night, fractured her hip, and developed pneumonia. She had lain on the driveway for a long time before anyone heard her cries for help.

Ray, the owner before Marna, had had Parkinson's. One spring, a fierce rainstorm tore through the neighborhood and flooded streets and yards. Everyone's house was safe and dry except Ray's. The storm flooded his basement and oil tank. The house needed environmental remediation and was unlivable for six months.

One day, out of the blue, Greg decided we should buy Marna's house. "I know I'm going to need a handicap-accessible bathroom and one-level living. I hate to leave our house, but at least we'll still be on the pond."

I was uneasy about the new house after we moved in.

"What is wrong with you?" he asked. "You need to calm down."

It's hard for me to tell my logical husband about how I began to fear this house many years ago when Ray owned it. I sense a growling energy in the house, and that energy makes me uneasy.

I wonder how to rid the house of the angry, broken-bone, flooding fears. I can live with my husband's challenges but not these spirits.

So, today, I will begin to tell the spirits that it's time to leave. They have to go bully someone else.

SLOW LOSS

Better yet, just settle down.

The swans are lost too. A swan mother left the pond last week and stood in the front yard for three hours. In my thirty-five years living on the pond, no swan has ever gone to the front yard and stood so silently. No hissing. No flapping her wings, no warning other creatures away. Was she sensing some house danger too?

Evil house spirits, we are all lost together.

It is OK.

The pond waters may rise, and we will be OK.

The ginormous sump pump will lull us to sleep, as comforting as the spring peepers in early spring.

We will live lightly like the chatty chickadees who love this house so much, always singing and bouncing from bush to bush.

On the darkest days of winter, we'll wear vivid colors, turn up Chaka Khan, and dance around the living room, that wide open space good for more than rollators.

"I feel for you," sings Chaka Khan.

I feel for you, oh lingering house spirits, but today you have to go, or you have to calm the fuck down. You might not know this, but I've stopped putting up with unnecessary drama and self-absorption, mine and other people's.

I feel for you, my own dear anxieties, my adventurous spirit that wanted to move to Providence, Vermont, Cape Cod, or Boston. Not two doors down to Marna's house.

The pond loves us and wants us to stay for a while.

Yesterday, our neighbors cut back some of the brambles and out-of-control shrubs to open up our view of the pond.

They are helping me see the love that is here. They are opening up space for that ugly energy to leave and for my neglected optimism to find a way to move in and settle down.

EVIL HOUSE SPIRITS

Goodbye, old house on the pond. Hello, new house. I am unpacking all the good energy and sweeping away the heaviness of loss, change, and the former owners' bad luck.

I will stand with the swan and revel in all that is weird and unusual, and then I will watch the winter sun set over Rawson Pond.

STORM AFTER STORM

The power has blown out in the new house.

Rain is pelting the roof, the windows, the driveway.

The new $15,000 generator sits against the garage, not yet hooked up. Two 120-gallon propane gas tanks sit sadly next to the generator. "Not yet, big boy," they seem to say.

The rain turns to sleet, angry and hard.

A branch falls off the maple tree and lands in a soggy spot in the yard.

The house is so quiet.

No furnace, no heat.

The pump that runs the septic system is out.

No humming from the refrigerator.

TVs, computers, iPads are all out of juice.

The utility outage app says no crews have been assigned.

Across the pond and up the hill I see streetlights.

Why do the people on the hill keep their power? Storm after storm we black out.

SLOW LOSS

The rain lets up, and I take the dog for a walk up the street.

Gas-powered generators growl outside some houses, straining to power a few basics like refrigerators and stoves.

The smaller houses are mostly dark and without generators.

A young, newlywed couple has candles lit on their fireplace mantel.

The big family across the street has a battery-powered lantern on the dining room table. It's like a fluorescent in-house lighthouse.

Branches are all over everyone's lawns, not caring if you're rich or poor, powered or out, candled or battery ready.

A gust blows up and there's an eerie, high-pitched howl, how an oncoming tornado might sound. Except I've never heard a tornado except in horror films.

Nor'easters are our windy villains.

Back at our dark house, I take off my crossing guard fluorescent vest. Undo the dog's leash. Put the poop bag in the trash. Pull down the heavy garage door.

The flashlight lights my way into the kitchen, across the living room, and into the bathroom. It leads me to Greg's room. He's asleep, yelling and laughing in his dreams.

When I place the flashlight on the bathroom counter, I see billions of dust mites and tiny bits of toothpaste. How have I missed those in cleaning?

I go back into the kitchen and lay the flashlight on those counters. It's a microbe mess. In the dark, I get out the white vinegar and start wiping things down. Then I bring out the bleach.

The neighbor's generator sputters, like it's exhausted, but catches its breath and goes on.

I undress by the windows in the dark and look out at the pond. Clouds are moving fast, blowing away the storm and letting the stars through.

STORM AFTER STORM

Now I see how midnight blue got its name.
I want to keep watching the sky.
I want to check the outage app to see if the repair crew has been assigned.
But this house with no lights and no heat is getting cold.
I climb into bed to wait.
For light.
For heat.
For morning coffee.
For power over the unpredictable.

PUT THE DOG DOWN

Today, we took our chocolate lab, Maia, to the vet. She's the dog we got right after Greg and Greg Jr. reunited ten years ago. Maia has been hard to discipline, but she's lovable, friendly, and smart.

She has always disobeyed the command, "Come." But when Greg tells her to run after the Canada geese and their goslings that are eating and pooping in our backyard, she takes off in a fury, chasing them until they fly away. She's also been known to use her retriever skills and pick up a gosling in her mouth and run back to Greg with her catch, wagging her tail.

Maia has been unable to eat for a week, vomiting out her insides.

Because he's sad and anxious, Greg's body is rigid, or frozen as it's called in Parkinson's disease lingo. He can't move and he can't get out of the car and come into the vet's office with me.

I put Maia on her lead, help her out of the car, and go into the office.

"We'll take a look right away and let you know what's going on," says the vet.

SLOW LOSS

She returns in ten minutes. "I am so sorry. Ordinarily, we'd give you a day or two at home to say goodbye, but Maia is suffering. We should probably do something immediately."

"OK. Let me see if my husband wants to come in and say goodbye to her."

Greg cries when I tell him. He can't move. He won't be able to have one last look into the brown eyes of his favorite dog and tell her how much he loves her. Loved her even more than Mookie, his first dog.

"Go. Just go. Don't make this worse by dragging it out," he says.

This decisiveness is not what happened with the first dog. His dog, not my dog.

What that first damn dog did twenty-five years ago is one of those vivid memories you never forget.

It was a warm Sunday afternoon. I pushed sixteen-month-old Ian into the red plastic swing attached to the elm tree in our backyard. He squealed and threw his arms up in the air as he went higher and higher. This was happiness.

Mookie, our malamute, sat at the base of the tree. He always thought he was my guardian. If I sat on the front steps, he sat beside me. When we stopped for a rest on a hike, he would sit by my feet, his green eyes watching what was going on around us.

Ian threw his special "lovey" on the ground. The lovey was an old cotton diaper that he liked to hold up to his face as he sucked his thumb. I turned around to pick up the lovey, and when I turned back, I saw the 120-pound dog lunge at Ian. I rushed in and grabbed the baby out of the swing. His head was bleeding through his hat.

PUT THE DOG DOWN

I ran into the house, screaming for Greg. Ian wailed in my arms.

"The dog attacked him. Oh my God. Get the keys. His head is bleeding. We have to get to the ER as fast as we can."

As Greg locked up the dog in its kennel and got his car keys, I untied the bloody hat and part of the baby's ear fell off.

"Here, hold him," I told my husband.

I put a towel around the Ian's head to try to stop the bleeding, put the piece of the ear in a plastic baggy, and we got into the car.

I did not use the baby car seat that day since I had my body wrapped around my son. His piercing cries were unlike any cry I had ever heard from him. The crying tore into my soul. "Please, dear God. Take care of this sweet child."

In the children's hospital ER, the plastic surgeon told us to go to the cafeteria. He said, "We're going to try to sew the ear back on, but we can't anesthetize the baby because he's so young. It will be too upsetting for you to hear him cry."

"You have to put the dog down," I told Greg over piss-tasting cafeteria tea.

"He didn't mean it. Mookie is like my child. Please, don't make me do this. Let's get through today and talk about it when we're not so emotional."

I wanted to throw the tea in his face. How could he be defending a dog? A dog that might have killed our son. A dog that had certainly caused permanent damage.

As we left the ER with the baby, the doctor told us to get rid of the dog. He looked at Greg and said, "I tell all new parents to get rid of their dogs when new babies come home. Dogs are territorial and protective of you. They view an infant as taking away their turf, especially an Alpha. This morning, we had a baby whose face was completely disfigured by the family pit bull. That baby is still in intensive care."

The reattached ear tip fell off my son five days later.

"Due to the nature of the ear's cartilage, it will be almost impossible to fix this," said the plastic surgeon. "As he grows older, and his hair grows longer, it will be unnoticeable."

Greg refused to put down the malamute or give him away.

"It was a one-off. He's not a bad dog. Please, please, just give this time."

I didn't tell any of my family or friends what happened. I was ashamed that I allowed that dog to live. I'm ashamed that while they thought I was this strong professional woman, I deferred to my husband.

Why did I put up with that? Why didn't I kick my husband out with his dangerous dog? Or pack up the baby and stay with my parents? Why didn't I call some service to take away the dog while my husband was at work?

A year later, the malamute ran through the electric fence and mauled and killed another dog—a dog also named Mookie. The traumatized owners of the dead Mookie said they wouldn't sue if we put down our dog.

"This isn't a discussion," I said. "Get that fucking dog out of here now."

Why am I putting up with his dementia denials now?

"I'm OK. You're exaggerating. You're the one driving me crazy. You're overreacting. If you put me in a home, I'll kill myself. Think about that," he says.

Some days, he's kind and appreciative. On other days, he's belligerent and mean.

Why am I putting up with another threatening situation? Not getting enough help. Not considering assisted living. Why have I been so passive? Is it good-girl Catholic guilt? Was it the training from my female relatives whom I so love and who so put up with men's bad behavior? Who made excuses and rationalized unpredictable, me-first men? Who always put themselves second? Whose denial refrain, like a Greek chorus, is, "whatever." No divorces in my family. Stand by your man.

Last night Greg, wobbly from PD and dementia, got up at 3:00 a.m. and shat in the shower instead of the toilet.

"Stop overreacting. It's easier to have diarrhea in the shower than the toilet," he scolded me.

As I scrub the shit off the tiles and mop the bathroom floor, I think of carrying my wailing baby to the ER, gripping that plastic bag with his ear. My husband and his disease are terrorizing me like that malamute.

I hear my dead mother's voice whispering to me: "You can do this. You can care for him. You are a strong woman."

"How could you have raised your daughters to be smart, fiercely independent women but teach us to accept bad male behavior?" I ask that mother's voice in my head. "Why didn't you yank your sister out of her miserable, alcoholic marriage? Why did you say your best friend was strong and brave because she was putting up with her narcissistic husband's mentally abusive behavior?"

She wasn't strong or brave. She was naïve and alone, trapped in an outdated belief system that expected wives to be dutiful, flexible, and accommodating. We were expected to soothe them when they were angry and keep the kids quiet when he was tired or hung over.

Mom, do you know your "successful" children have worn self-protective armor their whole lives, trying to control our lives and not let hurt in? Not to feel deeply about anything? We've obsessed over making money, avoiding conflict, burying emotions, denying children's alcohol issues, and ignoring signs of psychotic dementia.

Yes, we have excelled at helping others. We are responsible and dutiful. We are compassionate warriors, just not to ourselves.

My sister called me this morning to say she's divorcing her husband of thirty-seven years. "He told the therapist today that I was the problem, that he didn't even want to try to make it work. So, why have I put up with this for so many years?"

"We were taught to make our marriages work no matter what. Mom taught us to be fixers. She never told us some things can't be fixed. Sometimes you have to walk away. You are going to be OK."

I realize that for years when faced with anxiety, I have avoided conflict and procrastinated decisions. I don't want to live with this ache in my gut, worrying about what this disease might do next to my husband and him to me.

I cannot procrastinate. I need to get help.

HELP

I put off hiring help. I know I need it. People keep telling me this. I think about it several times a week. But I don't think we're there yet. Greg is mostly OK. I don't want to spend the money until we need to. Though Greg is ten years into this disease, the neurologist says he could live for another ten years or more. I have to make our savings last.

It also seems easier for me to invite Greg to run errands than to hire and manage someone to sit with him. Or, possibly, I don't know how to ask for help. Or admit I need help. Even more likely, I want to avoid Greg's reactions when I mention getting help.

"What, you want someone to come here and babysit me? What would this person do? Watch me listen to a book. I am not as bad as you think. You're the real problem. You worry too much."

Today, I decided we needed to go to Home Depot to buy cleaning supplies.

I love to clean my house, which is new since COVID and cutting back on work. My friends are shocked when I tell them about my obsession. I've learned cleaning formulas like Dawn dish detergent and white vinegar are good for cleaning almost everything. I've bought new tools, from telescopic dust wands to different-sized grout cleaning brushes. I've found cleaning checklists for every room so that you get the job done thoroughly.

"You're scaring me," says a friend. "Cleaning? You need to find something better to do."

When it comes to cleaning, I am as manic as Greg often is, and I don't have Parkinson's.

I know this is a control issue and a response to boredom. When I finish cleaning the kitchen, the stainless-steel appliances gleam, the hardwood floors shine, and the sinks and counters are crumbless and spotless. There are no cooking smells. No dust bunnies are hiding under the refrigerator or in that narrow little space between the stove and the counter. I am woman. I get shit done.

"Do you want to get out of the house and ride over to Home Depot with me?" I ask Greg.

He does. It takes a lot to get to the store, though it's just ten minutes away. Greg fills his fanny pack: extra medicine, wallet, phone, carabiners, eyeglass cleaner, Swiss Army knife. You never know what you might need, his paranoia brain tells him. I load his rollator into the trunk. He struggles with fastening his seat belt.

"Can I help you with that?"

"No, I'll figure it out."

The car idles and warms up as he tries once, twice, five times to put on his seatbelt.

"I forget how this works. Can you help me?"

We walk slowly through Home Depot. Greg puts a six-foot PVC tube into the shopping cart.

"What's this for?" I ask.

"I have an idea and might need this."

HELP

"C'mon, Greg, we just cleaned our old house out of "might need" stuff like this. Let's not start accumulating crap again."

"I need it." He puts three PVC tubes into the cart, a sort of f-you.

When we get home, I start to feel funny, like a boa constrictor is wrapped around my chest, squeezing tighter and tighter. My head hurts, and I rush to the bathroom, thinking I'm going to vomit. Is this what a heart attack feels like? My grandfather, grandmother, father, aunts, and uncles all had heart disease.

I look up heart attack symptoms on the Mayo Clinic website. I have every symptom. I decide to drive to the ER. My blood pressure is elevated, I have a family at-risk history, and I'm sixty-six. I'm so concerned about myself that I don't think about whether I should leave Greg alone.

Ten hours—and too many medical tests to recount—later, I walk out of the hospital and go home with a prescription for heartburn medicine. There is nothing wrong with me except for gastritis. The tests show I'm in excellent health for my age.

"So, it's all in my head?" I asked my doctor when she calls the next morning.

"Your pain is real, but the cause is anxiety and stress. Caring for your husband is more overwhelming than you're admitting to yourself. You should try to get away for a couple of days and get some help. Doctor's orders."

FAIRIES NEED TO FLY

Ian is home from Los Angeles due to COVID, and he has agreed to keep Greg company for a weekend, which means I can join friends for the Nantucket Stroll, a festive December event where people dress up in bad Christmas sweaters and party more than stroll.

My friend, who has a house in Nantucket, says we're invited to a party hosted by a renowned party planner, a woman who often does events for Oprah.

When we arrive, we wonder if we've dressed right for the occasion. The men wear custom-made Christmas suits. Some are plaid wonders. Others have matching pants and jackets adorned with Christmas trees, candy canes, and Santa. The less prepared or more frugal wear red velvet capes, green bow ties, and Santa hats.

The women wear holiday glam: red and green velvets, sequined halter tops, and silk palazzo pants. One woman looks like a snow queen with her rhinestone tiara and long white satin dress with white fur trim along the cuffs, collar, and hem.

SLOW LOSS

I wear a wreath of ivy, berries, and red ribbons, a one-of-a-kind Swarovski atelier necklace that I have never worn in the thirty-six years since my Swarovski client gave it to me, kitten-heeled suede booties, a sequined blouse, and my oversized, red-orange Land's End down jacket.

The party is jammed with billionaires, lawyers, party planners, inventors, teachers, new retirees, and mysterious people reluctant to reveal much about themselves. Most of us party outside, freezing with great frivolity. COVID be damned. We are vaxxed.

"You're like a wood nymph. How magical you are," a handsome guy in his forties says to me as we stand on the deck of the Nantucket cottage, drinking prosecco. It turns out he was one of the early organizers of the Burning Man Festival.

"Going out to the desert for Burning Man is on my bucket list," I say.

"Oh, you have to come to our camp. It is so perfect, especially for newbies. Tell me you'll come next year."

I swirl around the party and talk to strangers. I ask them questions about their outfits, their work, and their beliefs. When they ask about me, I tell them I am a wood nymph.

I like this label more than others that are often used to describe me. Wood nymphs have much more fun at parties than teachers, lawyers, corporate strategists, or even writers and artists. They are especially more fun than a caregiver.

"Should we be worried?" asks my friend who copped the invitation to this party of strangers. "There are so many people squished together, and no one is wearing a mask."

"Life is short. We're triple-vaxxed. Let's not worry tonight," I say and move on to another interesting stranger. We are still in Delta territory; Omicron won't be a thing for another week.

FAIRIES NEED TO FLY

I am an introvert who generally loathes cocktail parties with strangers. Tonight, I feel exuberant. Out, dressed up, learning fascinating things from people way outside my usual social circles. Has my costume turned me into someone else? Is it the joy of being at a party after almost two years of isolation? Or is it the freedom of being away from home for a couple of nights? I hope Greg will be OK.

I see my two friends, with whom I came to the party, hovering nearby, edging closer to me. A guy is saying to me: "I bet you've made at least a billion."

This is hilarious. Why would he think this? All I've done is ask him questions about himself. If only he knew I drive a Subaru, and my former summer house was not a multimillion Nantucket "cottage" but a White Mountains cottage with no running water and an outhouse.

But it's fantasy night. Let's pretend night. I let him think I've made more than a billion.

My girlfriends move in. "We're giving you the fifteen-minute warning. Then it's time to go."

Boo. They used to do this to me at college too. Maybe they shouldn't have played it safe tonight, sitting quietly by the gas fire with one group of people, dressed sensibly and spaced judiciously. Maybe then we could have stayed longer.

Finally, they tell me that the Cinderella wood nymph has to go to bed. That I will regret it if I stay any longer and drink more champagne.

We get back to the house, wash up, and get into our pajamas.

"Good night," I shout down from upstairs.

"Not yet," they say. "Let's have a cup of tea and debrief."

I tell them about the guy who helped start Burning Man and who christened me "The Wood Nymph."

"What is Burning Man?" they ask.

"Oh, my dear friends, you have to widen your world. It's a big deal. On my bucket list."

I tell them about the guy at the party who was the former chair of a famous museum, the intrigue and pettiness in the big-money art circles, and the workshop the former president of RISD and I did at said famous museum.

"We didn't think you knew anything about fine art," they astutely say.

"I don't, but I am a good facilitator and have found myself in some crazy worlds doing that kind of work."

During the party debrief, I realized how much I have missed leading a life of unexpected adventures, how much I have enjoyed saying "yes" to quirky people, places, and invitations, and how wistful and occasionally despairing I've become.

Back in my suburban mainland, I return to my cautious, dutiful life.

I test positive for COVID.

"You party, you pay," Greg reminds me.

A month later, I still can't eat sugar or have even a sip of wine without getting sick. Sometimes, my towels smell like cigarettes, and my duvet smells like gross burnt chocolate—all impossible smells.

I keep my ivy wreath perched on my dresser. When I feel especially felled by COVID or Greg's disease, I put on the crown and remember the party.

Fairies need to fly.

DURING: 2021

TIME TO GO

"When I think about you leaving, I think about how few times I may see you again in my life. Is it two? Three?" Greg asks our son Ian.

The beeswax candle is melting all over the table as we linger over dinner.

Tomorrow Ian goes back to Los Angeles with his girlfriend to resume his post-COVID career as a visual effects artist.

His car is packed. His smelly room downstairs is bare except for the olive green sleeping bag he's using tonight. Just twenty-four hours ago, that room was stuffed with computer monitors, pillows, a pile of clean clothes heaped on the other bed, empty candy wrappers crumpled up on his desk, and his little Buddha statue on the windowsill.

"I guess you won't be home for Thanksgiving or Christmas," I say to break the sadness, but maybe I'm just filling the room with more sadness.

"We'll probably go up to Oakland to see Jonah on Thanksgiving. Who knows about Christmas? Depends a lot on the new job."

"Of course. I know how much you want to get back into your work and life in LA with Ava."

SLOW LOSS

This creative son has been my partner in exploring cities, stand-up comedians, music, theater, and art.

I remember sitting at an outdoor café in lower Manhattan after an off-off-Broadway show one May when he was sixteen. As soon as school was over in June, he was going to hike the last 150 miles of the Appalachian Trail. Love of cities was from me, the wilderness from his father.

Ian's phone rang as we were about to eat after the show. It was midnight.

"Sorry, Mom. I have to take this for a few minutes."

He started speaking a language I can't place, this child who refused to take more than the required two years of high school Spanish.

He signed off and came back to our table.

"Well, that was fun," he says. "I had reached out to this guy in a Swedish folk metal band. He called me. Can you believe it? They're coming to Boston in the fall."

"Were you talking to him in Swedish?"

"Yeah."

"Where did you learn Swedish?"

"You can learn anything on the internet, Mom."

Now, ten years later, he is speaking of his love of the West—the mountains, the music scene, the ability to buy any kind of ethnic food within a ten-minute bike ride in his West LA neighborhood, the frustration of doing a project for a famous movie director, but Pink and Keith Urban were pretty chill, and the thrill of living with his girlfriend, Ava.

He will likely never return to New England. It's too small, too safe, too bland.

We wanted to raise an adventurous, kind, creative child. We have succeeded and lost him to worlds that are not ours. Or maybe we have freed him to be comfortable in worlds that are foreign to us.

TIME TO GO

I leave the house before he leaves for LA.
"Text me, OK?" I ask before going for a walk in the woods.
"Will do, Mom."
"Safe and sound in PA!"
"Checked into our room in Indiana."
"Home for the night in Missouri."
"Checked in! About 90 min. outside of Denver in eastern Colorado."
"Arrived in mid-Utah!"
"Amazing! Stunning views of the Rockies today. We stopped at a gear company in Leadville."
"Greetings from the 80-degree southern California desert. We're getting into our Airbnb in the morning!"
"We have arrived in Burbank!"
"We just toured an amazing place with a landlord instead of the property management company."
"We got the house! 4.8 miles via bike to get to work. Goes by the LA River and an equestrian center."

I close his texts and go to the local market to order a turkey.

"How many this year? Another big crowd?" asks the butcher.

Thanksgiving is our family's big holiday. Eighteen, twenty, thirty-five people at our house. Fold-up tables. Coolers on the deck. Too many cooks in the kitchen. Each person sharing what they're most grateful for this year. Somebody drinking too much wine. Someone else quietly cleaning up and scrubbing all the pots. And oh, so many pies. Apple, pumpkin, mince, pecan.

"No, just seven of us this year," I say. "Better than last year when we couldn't have anyone over because of COVID."

I try to put a smiley face on how sad I feel.

About our son.

SLOW LOSS

About our extended family who chose to travel or go elsewhere this year. Is being with Greg too uncomfortable? Or are they just catching up with people they haven't been able to see during COVID?

I want the family chaos.

I want the stress of figuring out where to sit everyone and cook everything with one oven and four burners.

I don't want to think about the fact that my husband can no longer eat turkey.

I want to be grateful for all I have and stuff the sadness somewhere.

"How many more times will I see Ian in my life?" Greg asks in a sad, slurry Parkinson's voice as I load the dishwasher.

"Who knows," I say. "Who knows?"

That was the last time Greg would see his youngest son.

WHAT ABOUT THE SONS?

What about her sons? She hasn't talked much about them. This isn't their story. She doesn't want them to be sucked into endings when they're in their beginnings. Greg Jr.'s new animal hospital in Miami is taking off, and Ian's career in LA is just starting.

Yeah, but their father is in tough shape. They should be around more to help.

She's trying to protect them. To remember their father's intelligence, adventurousness, and rational thinking. After all, her son only had about fourteen good years of him, and her stepson, his son, only had ten years of knowing his biological father before the PD kicked in.

I think she's dodging. Maybe those sons are avoiding the situation because they're self-absorbed, and she doesn't want to see it. Sometimes, she looks at the world with rosy glasses and blocks out reality.

Oh, my friend, you've got it wrong. These guys would do anything for her or their father. If she were to send out a family SOS, they'd be on the next planes home from LA and Miami.

I think they're being irresponsible, waiting for an SOS vs. being around more.

No. She's protecting them from the drama of their father's life so they can fully live their lives. Her friends, siblings, and career have given her such meaning and joy. She wants her sons to have that foundation too. She'd also like to see herself as a lighthouse, not an anchor.

Oh my God, did you really say that? I'm choking on the triteness of the metaphor.

Hey, you're the one who tells me that I should speak more plainly. My point is that she believes children are not meant to be their parents' saviors or indentured servants. Treat them that way, and they'll pull away. Parents, however, should be their children's saviors if something goes wrong. That's our responsibility.

So, no laying guilt?

No! Not even on yourself. As we age, we do our best and take care of our spouse and ourselves. But no laying guilt on anyone. It never helps anything or anyone. It's been a struggle for her, having grown up with all that oldest-child, Catholic good-girl guilt. But she's doing better than when he was diagnosed a decade ago. I overheard her say, "Guilt stunts growth" to a friend the other night after her second glass of champagne.

Oh, dear. Someone help her with the cliches. At least she has the sense to drink good champagne and knows her birds.

THE MAFIA DON

The Mafia don runs our pond.

He hasn't been around yet this spring. He usually lets everyone settle in, fluff their early spring nests, and birth their babies in May. Every year I hope he'll forget about this pond and won't come looking for his protection payments. Probably not.

The pond's spring cycle works like clockwork, a predictable pattern of our lives since we moved here thirty-eight years ago.

The peepers start singing exactly on cue between March 25 and 28. They have never disappointed us.

Then come the Canada geese, hundreds of them swarming the pond in late March, just after the peeper all-soprano choir. Now, in mid-April, it looks like there are twenty goose couples mating, staking out protected inlets where they'll sit on their nests.

The geese squawk at all hours. While the peepers are sundown to 10:00 p.m. partiers, the geese honk it up at 4:00 a.m., 2:00 p.m., 11:00 p.m., and whenever they damn well please.

I put up wire fencing to keep the geese and their voluminous gray poops off my lawn. They just fly over, eat the incoming grass, and honk at me when I run into the yard with my arms spread wide, screaming, "Get out! Get out!" The three-year-old next door thinks it's hilarious when the gray-haired lady runs around her yard like a human airplane, chasing the geese, stepping in poop.

The geese hop over the fencing and go back to the pond when they see me coming. When I return to the house, they just hop back into the yard.

Like the peepers, the ducks are respectful. Their quacks are gentle, like a xylophone to the geese's tuba. The ducks have the most babies, usually ten or twelve ducklings. Rarely do any make it to summer. The giant, old, snapping turtle gets most of them. And the Mafia don when he's in town.

The human pond dwellers text one another when the ducklings are born, sharing this year's count. We're all hopeful that maybe this year, more ducklings will survive. Our texts slow as the ducklings disappear.

The swans are the pond bullies. They are arrogant, hissing, and picking fights all day long with the geese. The ducks flee up the river when the swans start cruising around, all predator-like for their mating season.

Last year the swans went all out and kicked a goose couple off of their nests over on the island. The fight was ferocious. The geese lost one of their eggs before the swans settled in and took over their nest. I knew they were bullies, but this seemed kind of lazy. Build your own nest, Swan Boy.

As I sat in the Adirondack chair down by the waterfront yesterday, the swans started hissing at me like I was too close to the shoreline, THEIR shoreline. I hissed back. They eventually left.

I know they live here because of the don. They all do. Especially the blue herons.

Three years ago, a heron couple built a nest on a treetop on the island. They carefully constructed their nest from twigs on the top of the highest tree. It's about three to four feet long. When gale winds knocked down trees and power lines last summer, the nest held. As the big pine tree next door cracked and fell on the neighbor's roof, I looked out and saw the nest swaying in the trees. No damage.

Two herons are on that nest now. These long-legged, four-foot-high birds balance on the tippy-top of the trees, letting their four-pound bodies sway in the wind while staying steady.

This year's big pond news is that two more heron couples are building nests in the island treetops. They're creating a rookery commune. But why? Didn't they hear what happened last spring? Wasn't one of them part of the rescue mission?

Last June, an eagle soared in and landed in the heron's nest. The usually quiet herons screeched, flapped their wings, and jutted their bills defensively at the eagle. The eagle sat on a tree branch and looked at the eggs in the nest. The herons wailed like an out-of-tune orchestra cacophony. All of us human pond dwellers stopped what we were doing, picked up our binoculars, and watched in horror. This was more violent than the day the snapping turtle and swan attacked one another for hours. (The swan lost.)

The eagle pecked at a heron egg, a tasty lunch treat. The herons continued to wail, and miraculously, another heron swooped in from who knows where to help. They perched close to the eagle, adding to the cacophony. The heron parents flew to a branch even closer to the eagle, desperate to save their eggs.

The fight lasted two-and-a-half hours. Eventually, the eagle flew off, leaving some of the eggs. He only comes by every month or so to collect payment.

Naturalists say the eagles are like Mafia dons. They offer the herons protection from predators like foxes, raccoons, and fishercats. The herons put up with the don because he or she protects them.

Researchers on the southwest coast of British Columbia have found that some herons even seek out nesting bald eagles and build right next to them. Crazy. Without the don, things could be much worse for the waterfowl on our pond.

By the time the bullfrogs start their deep alto ribbiting in late June, the surviving heron chicks, goslings, cygnets, and ducklings are learning to fly. Everyone chills out in summer. The spring mating, birthing, and Mafia payment season is over.

By September, things will be quiet as the birds head south again. The only thing left is the empty treetop heron nests. The nests make the trees look like they are wearing bad toupees. Toupees fit for old Mafia dons.

Oh, Mother Nature, how we love you.

How we love days like this, where the don, not the disease, rules our lives.

ENRAGED BY PERKY ADVICE

Despite my willpower to ignore it, perky advice enrages me.

I'm in a funk about all that is happening in the world. Mass shootings. School book bans. Terrorism. Losing two feet of shoreline of Rhode Island beaches every year due to climate change. Opioid crises.

One of my go-to coping skills to snap out of a funk like this is to learn something new.

Today has been a challenging day of doctors' appointments. I go online and read "Finding a More Meaningful Life Through Caregiving."

"If he is living in 1968, enter into his reality and enjoy it. This isn't to pacify him. This is an opportunity to communicate and treasure memories out of time."

Are you kidding me?

How many times would you like to hear the same two or three treasured memories? Twenty, a hundred, every day for ten years? Forget out of time. I am out of my mind hearing about his time at Hunter Air Force Base and how big the NCR computers were back in the day. Hearing the same memories over and over again is like noise torture. Like I'm a prisoner of war being tortured with the repeated playing of heavy metal Metallica and the Barney theme song, which is what was used on Iraqi POWs, according to a BBC report.

I really should stop reading this. Look at the cheesy photographs of smiling people. It's hard to believe the guys in the pictures are losing their minds and that their brain cells are disintegrating. Look at them wearing those crisp, ironed blue oxford shirts, with full heads of styled hair, smiling attentively and looking alert.

Have you been in a neurologist's waiting room lately? People are leaning on their walkers, wearing shirts that snap because buttons are unmanageable. Their faces have blank, vague, emotionless expressions. This disease is tragic. Do not try to be cheery and delusional. We caregivers are not buying it.

And the wives in the booklet photos? Look at them fawning over their husbands, so patient, all soft edges. Their faces have wrinkles, but they look rested, like they sleep eight hours a night, like they have no backaches from getting someone twice their size up off the floor after a fall. I used to want to look like Audrey Hepburn did at my age. Now I want to look like one of these caregiver models. (Their hair is such a perfect color, and the bob is blow-dried perfectly. Gorgeous!)

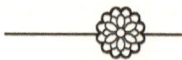

I turn the car radio to the local NPR station and the "This I Believe" segment. My mood turns from balanced to bitch-crazy angry.

"Many of us have known friends and loved ones whose minds and mental faculties have slipped away as some form of dementia has

ENRAGED BY PERKY ADVICE

tightened its unrelenting grip," says the local NPR announcer in an emotionless voice.

"We know the challenging signs: confusion about time and place, memory lapses, language difficulties, mood changes, isolation. No doubt, this is a painful, agonizing process for nearly everyone caught in its midst. But some of us also find precious, even bright moments as we travel this complicated journey. Jennifer has found just that, and in today's segment, she shares lessons she's learned."

Jennifer tells us about the unexpected pleasures of spending time with her eighty-five-year-old father who had Alzheimer's. Perky Jennifer tells us how her family gathered around and helped her dad. How sad it was when they had to move him into a nursing home. How she volunteered at a daycare center for dementia patients after he died, which turned into a whole new career path as a recreational director at a care facility (a.k.a. nursing home.)

This has been such a beautiful, life-affirming career change for Jennifer. Her dad would be so proud of her.

Go, Jennifer! You bitch.

If I were on the radio, I would tell my extraordinary caregiver sisters to tune out upbeat, superficial, well-intentioned people and propaganda. It's more delusional than our husbands' deteriorating brains. We're getting through each day. We're grieving. We're running a marathon we never trained for.

We need stamina and kind truthtellers, not perky cheerleaders. We need to be able to deal with reality and not become angry, anxious, bitter victims.

NAME EVERY SIGN

We're driving to the endodontist's office for the second time today. Greg lost the temporary crown that was put on this morning. If we can get to the dentist's office by 4:55, she'll put a new one on.

I know what's coming as I drive down Route One. Greg does this on every drive to every doctor's visit. I try to ignore it because it makes me crazy.

We stop at a red light, and he starts.

"Target," he begins.

Applebee's.

Sunoco.

Home Depot.

Pet Depot.

His Parkinson's dementia brain names everything we pass. Saying the names of familiar signs grounds him. Some days, I take back roads to avoid driving by businesses with big signs. It doesn't work.

Detour.

Children Ahead.

Dead End.

Yield.

If I ask him to stop, he gets more anxious.

I try to be more patient so that I can soothe him. I've read neuropsychology books that say emotions are contagious. If I become angry, annoyed, anxious, sad, or fearful, he'll catch it like a nasty virus. I try to suppress my emotions, especially anxiety.

I take a different route to the dentist this afternoon.

UPS.

CVS.

Exxon.

I can no longer ignore his naming each sign. Rather than scream, I join in.

Toyota.

Dunkin' Donuts.

Verizon.

"What are you doing?" he asks.

Jordan's Furniture, I continue.

Wal-Mart.

Marshalls.

I say every sign aloud, hoping they ground my sanity like they do his.

"Hey, are you messing with my brain?" he asks.

"I thought this is a game you like. Name Every Sign."

We're silent for the rest of the drive.

I don't want to be mean.

PLEASE, PLEASE, PLEASE

Dear God or Divine Guidance or Jesus, Mary, or Joseph: Please help me stay optimistic.

Please don't let me become bitter and brittle.

I struggle every week to be caring, patient, kind, compassionate, and a good listener like all the Parkinson's and Alzheimer's associations recommend. I struggle not to morph into a victim. But man, oh, man, some days are really hard.

His hallucinations are usually nice monkeys or children, but those snakes last week were violent. He threw his iPad across the room to "get 'em." He installed security cameras outside and inside the house.

He keeps accusing me of being the cause of all his issues and discomfort.

Then there's obsessive spending on sump pumps, hoses, and replacement parts for the sump pumps. We've never needed to turn the sump pump on. We now have three sump pumps installed. Jesus, please never flood our yard.

SLOW LOSS

Then there are the denials. "I'm fine," he says when I try to pick him and the rollator up off the floor at 2:30 a.m. This is not fine.

And, dear God, I hate that edge in my voice when we have visitors.

"Wow," they say. "He is doing great. I thought he'd be in worse shape after all these years with the disease."

"He is not doing great," I correct them. "You have no idea."

My response makes them feel uncomfortable. Maybe they think he's right when he tells them that I'm going crazy, not him.

Thank you, God, for sending me good friends who are going through the same things with their husbands. They've taught me so much, and they never judge my despairing outbursts and stories about what's going on with Greg and me.

I'm so sorry these friends' spouses have been sick for so long, God. They've told me about their angry, bitter years and how they're behind them now. These caregiver sisters are amazing people. Please, God, make me more like them. Help me get beyond this bitterness. The sooner, the better.

Dear Lois,

This is God. I've reviewed your many letters and want you to know that I have love rays beaming into your house.

I overheard you telling your sisters that you feel like you're finally settling into the new place, making it a home vs. a temporary place to live until he dies. This acceptance you're feeling is from one of the love beams. Remember last week when you thought the moon was lighting up the pond outside your bedroom windows? Those were my love beams.

In addition to the love beams, I'd like to suggest a few things.

PLEASE, PLEASE, PLEASE

I want you to let him go down to the cellar and play with his new sump pumps. Stop nagging him with "Be careful!" every time he goes downstairs. If he falls down the stairs, you call 911.

If he buys too many hoses and sump pumps, you eventually call JD Junk Dog, and they'll take them away in their trash trailer. No big deal.

I also want you to practice using a new word. Every time you mutter "fuck" loudly or in your head, replace it with "okey-dokey."

'Cause, honey, it will be okey-dokey. You've got so many good friends. You've got enough money to hire some help. Whoa, whoa, do I hear you pushing back on that statement? I know you worry incessantly about money, but there will be enough. Not gobs for National Geographic trips or a house in Woods Hole, but enough to hire help so you can get away for a couple of days.

Know that winter will be hard again. Your friends will be heading to St. John, Florida, Portugal. You'll be putting ice melt on the driveway.

I'm absolving you of all Puritan guilt about being lazy in the dead of winter. Read, binge on those series, sleep late. When you're rested, you're much less likely to be bitter.

You can do this, my love. There is nothing good about this situation with your husband. Know that I am not testing your goodness nor making you do penance for that which will not be written. It's just the end of life on Earth, the wearing away of minds and bodies. This is not to be feared.

Others will have their challenges, too, so don't think you've been called out in some special way. You're just walking through this earlier than your friends.

SLOW LOSS

You do know, I hope, that your friends have always looked up to you, especially your bravery. Show them how to bravely care for a partner. Let them in on the struggle for love over bitterness. You don't have to hide the ugly and put a smiley face on things. We don't give sainthood to martyrs.

Things will get worse—you know that. I am here for you, as are your sisters, cousins, friends, neighbors, and 911 EMS professionals.

Now go take a shower, put on your favorite fleece sweater, turn off the computer, and relax.

Okey-dokey?

Dear God,

Okey-dokey? For some reason, I thought you'd sound more dignified, like a British Shakespearean actor. But roger on the relaxing and not becoming oh-woe-is-me all the time.

Lois

DURING: 2022

A SPRING ALL-NIGHTER

"Tonight's the night," I text a neighbor.

I open my bedroom windows even though the temperature is still in the forties. I climb into my bed, pull the duvet around me, and wait.

Yes, there it is. The music is clear, high-pitched, and stereophonic. The spring peepers are singing.

Pureek, pureek, pureek. This call lasts about ten seconds. A higher-pitched new call echoes from another part of the pond, lasting almost twenty seconds. One male peeper trying to outdo another to win a mate.

I close my eyes and listen to the tree frogs' trills. I try to meditate and listen to the pond sounds.

Wait, what? Do I hear Greg in the kitchen? Why is he still awake? Breathe in and out. Listen to the peepers: Pureek. Pureeeeeeeek. Listen and relax.

SLOW LOSS

I must have dozed off. It's 1:00 a.m., and the outside floodlights are on. They light up my bedroom and our neighbor's bedrooms. I hear the freezer door open and the angry whir of the blender.

I get up from bed, turn off the outside lights, and go into the kitchen, where Greg is binge-eating junk food.

"You should go to bed now. Remember our agreement? No activities after dark?"

"I'm fine. Leave me alone. I get up in the middle of the night all the time, and you don't even know it."

"But remember what happened last week when you got manic and paranoid like this?"

"That's because Wayne died. That's why I was upset last week. Go to bed and leave me alone. You are overreacting."

Wayne was one of Greg's close friends. When the COVID lockdown started in March 2020, Wayne called Greg every week from his home in St. John. They talked about politics, history, nature, weather, and questions about God, the afterlife, and spirituality. I could hear Wayne ask questions and offer wise perspectives. There was no judging or advice-giving—just a friend's love and observations about failing health and the threat of death. Greg's brain was decaying; Wayne's heart and liver were failing.

Wayne often quoted Maya Angelou or Van Morrison's lyrics to provide context to his observations. His cadence had the magical rhythm of a poet or singer. It was calm and comforting. He had a poet's soul and a philosopher's mind.

"I've never been into music or read a lot of fiction, but I like these thoughts," Greg would say to Wayne. "Tell me more about them."

Wayne's wife, Rosanne, texted early last Wednesday morning to tell us that Wayne died while waiting for a heart and liver transplant. He was sixty-eight.

A SPRING ALL-NIGHTER

Greg's grief took the form of violent hallucinations that felt real to him. The imaginary Wayne was in Greg's bedroom but wouldn't listen to Greg; not like Wayne at all. Greg screamed, "Wayne, Wayne, why won't you answer me?" Then the hallucination faded. "Don't leave. Come back, Wayne." Greg slept the next two days, exhausted and bereft.

"I don't think I was this sad when my parents died. I loved Wayne so much."

So, yes, I see Greg's logic. Last week's delusional episode was probably a reaction to Wayne's death. And, yes, a lot of people get up and snack late at night when they can't sleep, like Greg is doing.

Chill, Lois, chill.

I lay down and try to stop my worrying by focusing on the sound of my beloved tree frogs. I count their mating calls.

The peepers start singing and mating the last week of March, without fail. Their joyful mating songs fill me with possibilities. They are announcing New England's seasonal rebirth. Soon the daffodils will be up, the trees will bud, the grass will become a fresh, pale green, and the neighborhood will come alive again as we emerge from our houses to walk, do yard work, and socialize. The days will get long and warm.

I have bundled up and sat on the back deck every year for the past thirty-seven years, listening and trying to figure out how many frogs are singing. I get so lost in the trilling that I often lose count. It's a wondrous night.

Tonight, I count the peeper calls as a tactic to manage my escalating anxiety. Not so wondrous.

At 2:30 a.m. I hear Greg yell. Not an angry or fearful "help me" yell. More like he's shouting over people at a party.

I get out of bed and go to the kitchen.

"What's going on?"

Greg has pulled liquor bottles out of the cabinets and lined them up on the kitchen counter, and he's taking pictures with his phone.

"Can't you see? It's a party. I can't believe how many people are here. Can you fix my phone? I keep taking pictures of people, but they're not coming out."

"Greg, I think you're hallucinating. These are imaginary people. That's why the pictures aren't coming out. Please come to bed."

"See what she's doing to me," he says to the imaginary people. He rocks from one foot to another, holding a bottle of Scotch as his dyskinetic arms flail around.

"Here, I'll put the bottle away. The party is over."

This is not the controlling Nagging Queen speaking. This is not the confident fixer and sprinter. This is fearful of me, knowing something bad is about to happen and I'm powerless.

This is the six-year-old me who acted as a foil as her grandmother shoplifted expensive clothes. I knew the drill. We would stroll into a fancy dress shop, and my grandmother would introduce me to the shop ladies, telling them how I was the understudy in the Metropolitan Opera's production of *Madama Butterfly*, that I got straight As, that I won first place in the Greater Boston art contest for first graders. This was my cue to start talking to the ladies and tell them about my adventures while my grandmother "looked around."

"Isn't she just so adorable," they predictably gushed.

Before entering a shop, my grandmother draped a large cardigan jacket over her arm. When we left a shop, she would take the cardigan off her arm, and the loot would be tucked neatly and discreetly underneath. After a successful "shop," she would take me to Zayre, a discount department store, and buy me a new outfit for my Barbie

A SPRING ALL-NIGHTER

doll. It was our Friday afternoon grandmother-granddaughter time together. "Our secret," she said.

I was always scared during these outings with my grandmother. I knew this was stealing. I knew this was wrong. I knew stealing was a big sin. I knew she never wanted me to tell anyone about our shopping. I loved her so much; she loved me and gave me special attention that I didn't get at home with all the babies. What would happen if she got caught? Would she get sent to jail? Would I be punished for not telling on her? If I told on her, would my Nanie stop loving me?

This is the same fear I feel tonight, sensing that something very wrong could happen. My chest constricts. The hallucinations have never been this complex.

"I can do this," Greg shouts, taking his phone back. "Let me take their pictures. You guys want your picture taken, right?" he says to his hallucinatory friends. Then he spots people who aren't supposed to be at the party.

"Why are those bad guys looking at me that way? They are outside, too, you know. That's why we need to keep the lights on all night and get more security cameras. I'm telling you: this house is possessed with people trying to get me to do crazy things to us."

I give up and go back to bed. Please, God, just a couple of hours of sleep. I need to sleep.

I can't sleep.

The peepers wind down and call it a night around 4:30 a.m., and the birds begin their shift. A new day. Moist soil. Worms galore.

It's no use. I can't sleep while he's like this. I get up and make coffee while he wheels his rollator around and around the house. Kitchen, living room, dining room, bedroom, bathroom, back to the kitchen and to the living room, dining room, bedroom, bathroom.

SLOW LOSS

Greg rolls through the house, talking and yelling at the invisible people chasing him.

At 6:00 a.m., the pond is quiet and still. The sun lights up the still-bare treetops with a blazing yellow-orange light.

I email the neurologist: "My husband has been awake for twenty-eight hours with acute hallucinations. What should I do?"

"Give him more Seroquel. It may make him very sleepy, but we need to get the hallucinations under control."

That was six hours ago. It's noontime and he's still going. A malfunctioning human Energizer bunny.

I call the neurologist. "Maybe you should bring him to the psych hospital ER so we can get him stabilized," he suggests.

No, a psych ER visit will result in hospitalization and worse symptoms. From my Parkinson's support group and late-night Google searching, I have learned the golden rule of neurological caregiving: No hospitals. Hospitals will only increase the person's anxiety, and the hospital is unlikely to follow every three-hour medication schedule most advanced Parkinson's patients need. Without the meds, their bodies become still and paralyzed, and their paranoia increases.

There is no cure for this disease. There will be no comfort for him at a psych hospital. I give him more meds.

The next day Greg is better, back in the land of the sane.

He leaves this note for me.

"We flew so high that this depth is much deeper.
Much is beyond my control, but I'll use whatever sanity
I have left to make your peepers sing for you.

Love, G.

DISTRACT ME, LOVES

I want to be distracted.
Not distracted like when you're trying to get ready for ten relatives who are unexpectedly stopping by for lunch, and you see three dead flies in the overhead bathroom light and wonder, "Should I clean that light before I run out to the store and buy cold cuts and ice cream?"

No, I don't want to be dead-fly distracted.

I want to be beautifully distracted.

This will be challenging for me. I am known as a fiercely disciplined person. When I get fixated on a project, I can work for hours. I forget to eat, ignore texts, and block out any thoughts unrelated to the task.

When I worked in the corporate world, I never knew about office romances, takeover rumors, or raging office debates over whether flavored coffee should be allowed in the lunchroom. No, I was in my corner office figuring out stuff, disdainful of those who missed deadlines. "Focus. Turn off your notifications," I wanted to lecture. The high I got from completing something complicated, thorny, and financially lucrative blinded me to all else.

I don't want to write about my current life situation. I want to escape from it because it's complicated and thorny, might bankrupt me, and is something I can't solve no matter how much discipline I bring on.

"Consider this doctor's orders," said my primary care physician on Friday. "Read Tara Brach's book, *Radical Acceptance*, and plan to get away at least once per quarter. I'm serious about this. The stress is eating away at your stomach."

I bought the book but haven't started it. Radical anything sounds like so much work.

I plan to figure out how to get beautifully distracted from my life. What if I researched and wrote about odd questions and curiosities?

Like why can't doctors' waiting rooms be quiet and beautiful? Why don't we wear floral wreaths every day at every age like the Romans? Why can't we have beautiful light-filled apartments overlooking greenery and parks vs. parking lots?

So, dear Creativity, you're going to have to help me unearth my curiosity. It's buried somewhere around here.

And Discipline? I need you, too, as I haven't been following through on much these days except dealing with the shitstorm of the day.

Please, dear ones, take me somewhere this month. Distract me. Pamper me. Help me escape in ways that feel regenerative vs. slothful. Give me assignments that challenge and immerse me. Please show me the beauty in exploring what is beautiful and unknown.

During a 2005 interview with Krista Tippett, Mary Oliver said she was saved by the beauty of the world.

Beauty, Creativity, Discipline: Save me, loves.

THE POW SIGNS IN

"Hold still, look up. There, that's the last of the eye drops until the morning."

I wipe the dribbling eye drops off Greg's face, put a pillow under his legs, and make sure there's a clean urinal hanging from his bed rail.

"What about my pills? Did you give me my pills? I think you've been getting them wrong. I think this is happening to me because you're making mistakes."

"I already gave you your pills. Try to sleep now. It's going to be an early day tomorrow. I'll wake you at 5:00 a.m. The sun should be coming up by then."

I lay in bed, unable to sleep. Tomorrow, he's having cataract surgery on his left eye. The right eye will be two weeks from now.

Maybe if he can see more clearly, he'll be more stable. He'll be able to read and use his camera. Might fuzzy vision have any correlation to hallucinations? Should I take something to sleep?

"This is an easy procedure," the ophthalmologist's assistant explained again yesterday. Ten, fifteen minutes at the most. Drop your husband off at 7:30 a.m., and we'll call you after we've given him all the postop instructions in the recovery room.

"My husband has advanced Parkinson's disease and dementia. I need to be with him. He won't understand the instructions."

"Oh, I see. Do you have a power of attorney? Good, bring that, and maybe they'll let you in. And by the way, if he gets restless and moves around, we won't be able to do the surgery. He needs to stay still."

Didn't I tell her he has Parkinson's? I hope for the best. My mood is positive. It's May. The days are long and warm.

I load the rollator, cane, extra Depends, and extra medicines into the trunk and then help him into the car at 6:00 a.m. Easy-peasy. So far, so good. Maybe my anxiety is unfounded.

When we arrive at the surgical center, the first step is paperwork.

"You have your power of attorney with you? Good. Now sign here and put POA next to your name. And here, and here, and just a few more. Good, you're all set."

I put on a mask over his face and mine, hairnets over our heads, and slippers over our sneakers. We head to the preop room.

"I'm freezing up. I need more medicine," he says, struggling to pick his feet off the ground more than an inch or two.

"I just gave you some. Give it a few minutes, and you'll be OK. If I give you too much, you'll get dyskinetic. If you move too much, they can't do the surgery."

He can't move his feet or turn around to sit in the recliner in the preop room. His anxiety about this procedure has frozen his body upright, rigid as a dead tree.

One nurse pushes the recliner's footrest down and out of the way. Two other nurses take one of his arms. They gently turn him around and coax the decaying old tree into the recliner. I play cheerleader.

"You're just about there. Feel the chair on the back of your legs? Good, good. Now just sit. Lower your bum. You've made it!"

THE POW SIGNS IN

Although we arrived early for the 7:30 surgery, eleven people are waiting ahead of my husband in the preop room. We're two hours into the tick-tocking of the depleting dopamine medicine. The greater the stress, the faster his body depletes the medication.

"You can take a seat in the waiting room now, Mrs. Matta. We'll call you when he's out of surgery."

I have a novel with me, but I can't concentrate. I start mindlessly browsing The RealReal shopping site and wonder whether I should buy the silver sandals for weddings this summer. But will I be able to go to the weddings? It's hard to get caregiving help for a Saturday and Saturday night. These sandals, though. The one-and-a-half-inch heel would be perfect for dancing. Before I can hit "buy," my phone rings.

"Mrs. Matta, this is Debbie the nurse. Could you come back to the preop area? Your husband is having some problems. Nothing serious, but we could use your help."

Greg is in distress. "I can't move. My legs, my legs. They're out of control. Get me out of here. Get me out of here. I can't do this."

"How much longer until surgery," I ask the nurses. "I can give him more meds, but they won't last long."

"We should have bumped him to the head of the line," a nurse says to her colleague.

"Let's do it. Put him next. Mrs. Matta? Could you stay here so that you can help us with your husband when he comes out of surgery?"

I sit on a swivel stool and wait. I peer over at his paperwork on the nurses' desk and see that I signed POW next to my name instead of POA, power of attorney. I have identified myself as a POW twelve times this morning. Every form has POW next to my signature.

Prisoner of war.

SLOW LOSS

I remember visiting Hoa Lo Prison in Hanoi, the infamous "Hanoi Hilton," where U.S. prisoners of war were held for almost a decade in brutal conditions. The signs at the Vietnamese museum say that the prison was "a serene time for these American pilots to think about what happened and feel the beauty of a peaceful life and warm humanity in Hoa Lo Prison."

Bullshit. That's like people telling me, "You can live a wonderful life with Parkinson's." There's nothing serene or beautiful about being a caregiver POW.

I remember hearing Navy Admiral James Stockdale talk about what he learned as a POW in Vietnam. He said the POWs who resisted reality and deluded themselves that they'd be home by Thanksgiving or Christmas became sick, and many died. Anxiety killed them. Instead of accepting what they couldn't change, they fought it through magical, delusional thinking. Every time one of their dreams failed— "We'll be out of here by New Year's, for sure,"—they lost part of their soul.

Stockdale said those who survived developed the ability to accept and experience their brutal reality and hold onto faith that they would prevail. They didn't let anxiety eat them alive.

"I never doubted that I not only would get out, but also that I would turn the experience into the defining event of my life," he said. I am putting my faith in Admiral Stockdale this morning.

When it's time for Greg to be discharged, his body is frozen and rigid again. It takes four nurses and me to get him from the recliner into a wheelchair and another ten minutes to fold his rigid body into the car.

"Do you have help at home?" a nurse asks as I close the passenger door.

"I'll be OK. Thanks for your help today," I say, like a confident Navy jet pilot preparing to fly over Southeast Asia in the late 1960s.

THE POW SIGNS IN

I am a POW. I know I will prevail and live to tell about it.

That night, I went online and bought a new bathing suit. Oops, online shopping is one of my bad habits when I feel anxious. Who cares tonight? A new bathing suit gives me optimism that I may be able to get to the beach this summer.

Today was rough, but I can do this.

To get to sleep, I whisper the Loving-Kindness Meditation.

"May you be happy.
May you be healthy.
May you be at ease.
May you be free from harm."

Then I say it for Greg, with some modifications.

"May you be happy.
May you be comfortable.
May you be free from harm.
May you have more good days than bad.
May your hallucinations be friendly."

Whatever happens next, I can handle it. Breathe in, breathe out. One foot and then the next. Feet kissing the ground, as Buddhist monk Thich Nhat Hanh would say.

Stay focused on the now. Let go of worry and let the tree peepers sing you to sleep. The day is done.

HIS BIG BREAK

"Lois. LOIS! Help. My legs are going crazy," Greg yells as the night turns into day. He has been up all night, walking from one end of the house to another with his rollator, unable to calm the pain in his legs. The anxiety of yesterday's cataract surgery has triggered a psychotic episode. His Parkinson's brain is sliding fast.

"Here, sit down. Let me give you some medicine, and you'll feel better."

He sits in a Windsor chair at our old farm table. The 5:00 a.m. sun is lighting up the treetops across the pond. It's supposed to be the first day of summer, reaching eighty degrees.

Greg begins to nod off in the chair, his head dipping to his chest, his right-hand fingers moving like they're signing a message to his hallucinatory friends and foes.

"Let's get you to bed so you can finally get some real sleep in a more comfortable position."

"I can't get up. My legs won't move."

"We can do this," I coach.

He rises and falls back into the chair one, two, five, six times. On the seventh try, he makes it up and grabs onto the handles of his rollator. I gently guide the rollator toward the bedroom as he takes his tiny, tentative steps.

"Stop," he commands. "You're going the wrong way. You're pulling me too hard."

"I'll go more slowly. This way. We're almost there."

When we get to the bedroom, he can't sit. He's rigid and frozen. He is standing up, his hands clenched on the rollator handles.

"What's going on?" he asks.

"The medicine hasn't kicked in, and you're frozen."

I push his shoulders, but he's stuck. Finally, his bum lowers to the very edge of the bed. He's about to fall to the floor.

"Can you scoot in a little bit so I can get your legs up?"

"What's going on?"

I lift his deadened legs, but they're hanging off the bed.

"WHAT'S GOING ON? WHAT ARE YOU DOING TO ME? GET ME OUT OF HERE! NOW!" he screams.

My husband has flipped from a kind, sick man to an agitated, angry beast.

"Who are you?"

"Greg, it's me. Lois. Your wife."

"What's going on? What's going on? Who are you?"

He starts to slip off the bed to the floor, his 210-pound body too much for me to lift.

I remember what the doctors told me, "If you think he may harm himself or you, call 911."

I don't want to call 911. I can do this. If he goes to the hospital, he'll get worse.

I call 911. Two police cruisers, a fire engine, and an ambulance descend on our quiet house.

"Sir, sir, what's your name?" asks the EMT.

HIS BIG BREAK

My husband looks up. "What's going on?"

"Who is this person?" they say, pointing to me. He looks at me intently, like my face is an unknown puzzle, and replies to the EMT: "What's going on?"

I tell them what hospital we need and ask them not to speed, blare the siren, or talk much in the ambulance.

"Please, be as calm and quiet as you can be. Any additional anxiety is going to make him much worse."

"What's going on?" Greg keeps saying as they strap him onto the stretcher. It's like all language has left him except for these three words.

I wish I could tell him what's going on. End-stage disease. Irreparable neurological decay. His worst nightmare.

The ER is a blur of paperwork, urgent tests, and shift changes. I am armed. I have a list of every medication, dosage, time of day to be given, and prescribing physician. I have multiple copies of his red MOLST document, Medical Orders for Life Saving Treatment, which my husband and his doctor drew up together five years ago. His instructions: don't do anything to save my life.

I tell the nurses that he needs medications every three to four hours or he will be in extreme pain, and he needs antipsychotic medicine twice a day and whenever he starts hallucinating.

"We'll do the best we can," says an exhausted nurse who works sixteen-hour shifts. Two hours later she tells me that the pharmacy doesn't have the medications. "Maybe you could go home and get them?"

I speed up Rte. 95, throw every prescription in a tote bag, and speed back to the hospital. I have only been gone seventy minutes, but arrive finding my husband in restraints, screaming, howling. "Get these fucking things off me. NOW!" he screams, yanking his arms and trying to get out of the restraints, rattling the bed rails with the strength of a much younger, healthier man.

SLOW LOSS

Without the medication, my husband goes berserk. The hospital has an ER "watcher" sitting with him because they have labeled him "dangerous, possibly suicidal."

"He just needs his medication," I say.

"We have to wait for the pharmacy to come down and approve your bottles," says the nurse and the watcher.

I put my hand on Greg's arm and try to soothe him.

"Get off me. Get me out of these. Oh fuck. Oh fuck. Oh fuck. Won't you help me? They won't help me. You have to help me."

Thirty minutes go by, and no one from the pharmacy comes. The watcher tightens the restraints.

"Would it be possible for you to get me a ginger ale," I ask the watcher.

"Of course," she kindly says.

As she goes to the refrigerator in the hall, I sneak Greg his medicine.

The case manager comes by next with a list of skilled nursing homes approved by the state.

"You need to start making some decisions. No memory care assisted living facility will accept him due to his physical needs, and I also think we'll have to consider skilled nursing with dementia secure units because he is so agitated. I'll work with you, but you need to give me five choices, and then we'll see who might have availability or accept him," she explains.

"Get me out of here. Oh fuck. Oh fuck. Oh fuck" plays in the background. The beast moans and roars in outrage.

I get the doctor to give my husband a sedative and ask that the restraints be taken off.

"I'm here. He will be OK."

Once the restraints are off, he holds my hand and more quietly chants, "Oh fuck. Oh fuck. Oh fuck."

"I will take care of you. Do you know who I am?"

"You are my wife."

Oh, thank God. I still have him.

The hospital decides to admit him, the sedation kicks in, and I leave at 10:00 p.m.

The psychiatrist calls me early the next morning. "Your husband keeps saying that he wants to die. That he thinks he hurt you badly yesterday. Did he? Do you think he wants to die?"

"He frightened me because the hallucinations got violent, and he didn't know who I was or where he was, but he would never harm me."

"Do you have guns or other firearms in the house?"

"God, no. We've never had guns in the house."

"I understand. It's just something we must ask when people are suicidal and depressed. The good news is that he is lucid, and the nurse says he's much better than last night."

I arrive at the hospital an hour later, and my husband is wearing what looks like white boxing gloves, and they are bloody.

"He tried to rip out his IV again, and we thought these would be better than the restraints," says the same CNA who was on duty last night.

"Get these OFF me. Please, I'm begging you," he says to me.

"Why are they bloody?"

"Because I was biting them with my teeth to try to get them off. My teeth are bleeding."

He is lucid but angry. He then says something that shocks me. Something he's never said in our thirty-nine years together.

"I'm so sorry I was mean to you in our marriage. I'm so sorry that I'd get mad and refuse to have sex with you for months. I'm so sorry I didn't go to your grandmother's funeral. I am so sorry for working too much. Please don't torture me by keeping these things on me. Take them off. I am so sorry. Don't be mean to me. I don't want to be mean."

I take off the boxing gloves and rub his legs.

"I am in so much pain. Why won't anyone help me with the pain? Oh fuck. Oh fuck. Oh fuck.

"The psychiatrist told me that you said you want to kill yourself. Is that true?"

"I'm not going to kill myself, but I can't live like this. I want to die."

"I know, it's so hard."

"No, you don't know. And you don't know that I have a loaded gun in my closet."

"What?! What are you talking about?"

"It's in my old briefcase with the computer, underneath the boxes on the top shelf. I don't want to hide anything from you anymore."

The nurses tell me that they're going to transfer him to a room for acute care. I can visit him tomorrow at 2:00 p.m.

"But what if he's agitated? Or not getting his medicine. I need to be with him."

"You'll have to see if they will make an exception."

I drive home, get a step stool, and climb into his closet to get the computer case.

I take the loaded Smith & Wesson, a gun cleaning kit, and three boxes of bullets and drive to my brother-in-law's house to ask him to get rid of it. I have no energy to go to the police.

What do I do tomorrow? How do I get into the hospital early? How do I ease his anxiety? Make sure he's getting the right pain and psych meds? What other surprise revelations might he share now that he is thinking about endings? Why did we hide so much from one another? How do I help him get out of his life with compassion, no restraints, and forgiveness?

HIS BIG BREAK

"No one should have to die in pain," say all the end-of-life articles. Maybe for cancer. But for these neurological terrorist diseases? For the lost years of marriage where we hid our simmering frustrations in the closet?

Oh fuck. Oh fuck. Oh fuck.

I LOOK AT THE PICTURE OF THE GUN

"I don't think I can do this anymore," I tell my sister, a geriatric nurse practitioner. "I need to find a good assisted living facility for Greg."

"You do. You're making the right decision."

"But what about the money? People can live a long time with Parkinson's. What if I run out of money?"

"This is the right decision. Don't worry about the money."

This is the first time in our lives that one of my siblings said, "Don't worry about the money." We have always worried about money, my three sisters, two brothers, and me.

We worried about being the only kids in elementary school who didn't have milk money. What would we do if everyone except us got their little carton of whole milk and graham crackers at the 10:00 a.m. break? How embarrassing would it be to sit at our desks with nothing because Mom couldn't send in money that week? It would be much worse than wearing hand-me-downs and not being able to play softball because last year's sneakers didn't fit.

SLOW LOSS

Why did my father drink at night, using the money that was supposed to pay for school milk? Why couldn't he be more responsible like the other fathers in the neighborhood and come home every night for dinner instead of going to the bar? Why did my parents have to fight over money all the time?

We worried about getting through college. Loans, grants, work-study jobs, and two jobs during the summer break. No spring break trips, new clothes, or free time. Free time meant we could be working. What do you want to do for a living? Something where we can make a lot of money because we never want to live like this. We never want to worry about money again. Never. What would you *like* to do? Doesn't matter. How much does it pay?

We worried when the sheriff boarded the door to our house because my father hadn't paid the taxes on his small tire store. We cleaned out our recent postcollege savings accounts and gave the money to my parents so they wouldn't lose their house.

All six of us bought houses as soon as we could and paid off our mortgages as soon as we could. All other expenses and pleasures could wait. We never wanted to worry about losing our houses.

I know I am falling apart and can't care for my husband at home. His PD brain is too out of control. I don't care what it costs.

I say this over and over: I don't care what it costs.

I think about the gun that was in his closet. Why did he only now tell me he had a loaded gun in his closet? Why did he tell me when he was restrained in the hospital bed, yelling he wanted to die? Would he ever have used the gun to hurt himself? Did the hospital psychiatrists think he was suicidal?

I think about the Smith & Wesson. It was heavier than I imagined a gun would be and beautifully made, a real work of artistry. It reminded me of some venomous snakes: handsome, regal, mesmerizing, and potentially dangerous, just like my husband.

I took a picture of the gun before asking my brother-in-law to get rid of it. When I worry about money and waiver about moving Greg into assisted living, I look at the picture of the gun.

Yes, it's dangerous for a person with psychotic dementia to live at home. I want to live. I want to amputate my hard edges calcified from fear, sharpened with the desperate need to try to control everything.

I want to be that joyful, grateful, hungry woman in the Skye teashop calling for more fudge cake. The woman who ran off for a month with her husband without worrying about money. The woman who loved her husband's calm, sensual voice, not his hallucinatory screaming or his reciting store signs as we drive by them.

I find an assisted living facility with an apartment available, but it is the most expensive apartment. I want my husband to be comfortable, to feel loved, to not be angry with me for this decision. Please, please, don't hate me, Greg. It would be worse than having no money.

I look at the photo of the gun and sign.

MAKING A MOVE

"This is mine?"

I've worried about this day for a month—two weeks while Greg was in the hospital and two weeks while he was in a rehab facility.

I have replayed every conversation we've had since he was diagnosed with Parkinson's eleven years ago. "I'd rather be dead than live in one of those assisted living facilities. Don't let what happened to my mother happen to me. Please, promise me this."

Greg's mother suffered from Alzheimer's disease for more than twenty years and spent eight years in a nursing home.

Greg has been clear about what he wants. No feeding tubes. No CPR. No life-saving surgeries. When he filled out the MOLST (medical orders for life-saving treatment) form with his physician five years ago, he placed a bold check mark next to "Comfort measures only."

"Don't even think of putting me in a place like my mother lived. We can manage this. I'm much better than you think I am," Greg has repeatedly told me over the past two years. "You're a much bigger problem than me. You need to get better at relaxing and not worrying so much. You're making me crazy."

So much anger, so many accusations, coming from both of us, at one another. In raging against the disease, we've raged against each other. Can we find our way back to tenderness? Or will today end all possibilities of that?

Will he yell at me, insisting that he's fine, and demand to go home or else he'll kill himself or leave me? Will I get detached and icy and speak to him like he is a misbehaving child? Will he turn cold and tell me to go, get out? "Are you satisfied now? Dumping me off so you can get on with your life."

I'm exhausted from playing out how this move-in day may go. Let's just get it over with. We walk into the assisted living apartment.

"Let me show you around. This is your bedroom."

"All my furniture is here, and the red blanket I like."

"Yes, and the bed has a new mattress."

"I've wanted a new mattress for a long time."

"Here's the walk-in closet and the bathroom."

"I love that shower and the built-in seat. Whoever put up the handicap grab bars knew what they were doing. They're mounted in the right places."

"Now for the part you're really going to like."

He turns his rollator around and follows me down a short hallway into a large, 12 ft. x 16 ft. corner room with a wall of tall windows overlooking the Providence River. Sailboats, kayaks, and the Brown crew team are on the water. Across the river, we can see the Providence skyline.

I have decorated the living room with modern, bright furniture that he can easily get into and out of. In less than a week, I found people to help me move his bedroom furniture from home to here; bought and assembled apple green, midcentury, plastic molded chairs from Target; convinced a furniture dealer to sell me a round white pedestal table for twenty-five dollars; bought new dishes and elegant plastic glasses for the kitchenette; enlarged, framed, and hung three of his favorite family photos— including our prom photo; and moved and organized his favorite clothes, shoes, canes, and devices.

However, my proudest accomplishment comes from what I found in the assisted living facility's storage and shipping area. It is a piece of furniture Greg has wanted for three years, but I have resisted buying it for our home because it is too much. Too big, too ugly, too heavy. It is a design monstrosity that screams, "The end is near, and it's not going to be pretty."

I saw it as I moved Greg's furniture in through the maintenance and receiving entrance.

"Excuse me. Hi, I'm Lois, and my husband is moving into an apartment on the second floor. Is this someone's chair?"

"No, someone moved out, and we need to get rid of that," says the maintenance manager.

"Could I buy it?"

"Buy it? You'd be doing us a favor by taking it. We'll get it cleaned up and move it upstairs."

My husband looks at this bulky, ugly monster of a chair and smiles.

"Mine?"

"All yours."

He sits in the powder blue lift recliner, presses a button, and the chair hums and tilts him into a reclining position. He presses another button, and the recliner tilts forward, lifting him into a standing position.

"I've always wanted a chair like this."

He admires the tilt recliner like he admired his new black Ford Bronco thirty-eight years ago. He walks around it, touches it, examines its engineering, checks for imperfections, and decides it's perfect.

SLOW LOSS

He is the happiest I have seen him in two years. All my worrying about how he might react to moving into this apartment was for naught. I feel my body relaxing and the "what's going to happen today" tension evaporating like iridescent soap bubbles, rising, glistening, and gently popping. Poof goes the anxiety.

"Is that India Point Park across the river? Could we walk there?"

"Of course, and there's also a small park on this side of the river. See, it's just down the street. We could walk there now if you want. Or we could sit outside and have something to eat on the porch. It's such a beautiful summer day, a ten-out-of-ten day."

Greg's not sure he believes me. We find the nursing supervisor.

"Can I just walk outside and go where I want?" Greg asks her. He thought he would be confined to this apartment like he's been confined to hospital and nursing home rooms for the past month. Until physicians could get his paranoid psychosis under control, he was in lockdown.

"As long as you sign out and wear the pendant around your neck, you can do anything you want to do," explains the nurse. "This is assisted living, not a nursing home or a memory care facility."

It is summer, and we are relieved, happy, and giddy that the psychosis, hospitalization, and depressing skilled nursing rehab stay are over. He has landed in a beautiful spot in the city we love, on the water, by the East Bay bike/walking path. The only available apartment was one with so many windows overlooking the water, just like home.

He is free, with no restraints, no chaos of the smelly nursing home and a roommate's large, loud family visiting, no hallucinations attacking him, no me nagging him 24/7.

"You're better," he says.

"Yes, I am. Much better. We both are."

TRULY PISSED

"Do you want to use the bathroom before we leave?"

"Yes, I better try. Just to be safe."

Greg and I leave the oral surgeon's office after a consult appointment. His teeth are disintegrating from taking so many medications. Dopamine. Antidepressants. Antipsychotics. Incontinence. Muscle spasms. Low blood pressure. B12 deficiency.

"Make an appointment for next week. This will be an easy tooth to pull," explained the oral surgeon. "You'll be in and out in ten minutes. No big deal."

Easy for him to say. Greg's cataract surgery was supposed to be ten minutes too.

Greg wheels his rollator out of the office. I help him into the car, fold up the rollator, lift it into the trunk, fasten his seat belt, and then mine.

"Is there anything you want to do while we're out?" I ask.

He hasn't left his assisted living center since he moved in three months ago. Going anywhere creates anxiety. The anxiety stiffens his muscles, which slurs his speech, paralyzes his ability to move his legs, and occasionally results in choking.

SLOW LOSS

Today feels OK. It's an easy appointment. A sunny, unseasonably warm day. Little traffic.

"Let's drive down to India Point Park. I think there's a big schooner docked there. I'd love to get a picture of it."

I drive onto the bayside road, watching for pedestrians, looking for the schooner, and eyeing places to park.

"There, there," he says. "You missed it. You went right by it."

"No worries. I'll turn around, drop you off, and find a place to park."

"No, no, no. You missed it. The boat's pulling out. It's too late. Just keep going."

"How about we drive down to Bullock's Point," I suggest. "There are beautiful views of the East Bay from that park. Maybe we'll catch a view of the schooner making its way down the bay."

"Do whatever you want."

About a mile down the parkway, Greg starts shouting. "Stop. Stop the car. NOW."

I swerve into an overlook parking lot along the bike path. People are unloading baby carriages and bikes. A historical group is gathered for a lecture about the Indigenous history of this piece of land. There's an open spot in the handicapped parking area.

In a blast of agility, Greg gets out of the car by himself and stands facing the busy parking lot.

"What are you doing," I yell as I run around the car to him, hoping he won't fall.

"I am peeing my pants."

Piss runs down his legs, dripping into his sneakers, drenching his shorts.

"There's a lot of it," he says as the urine pools in the parking area. "I couldn't go at the dentist's office."

"Let me help you into the car and get back to The Tock," I say with my patient voice. "I have a towel I can put on your seat. It will just take a couple of minutes to get back."

As I go to get the towel out of the trunk, he starts pulling down his shorts and Depends.

"No, not here. Look at the people. Please get into the car. Let me pull your pants up," I plead.

He refuses. He stands rigid with his seventy-four-year-old sagging balls hanging in public despair. He is trapped by the wet Depends and shorts moored around his feet. I go back to the trunk, pull out an old sheet, and hold it up around him. But how can I get his Depends off and pants on if I'm holding up the sheet?

I turn him around so that he faces into the car and tell him to hold on to the open door. I go back to the trunk, get some bungee cords, and use them to attach the sheet to the car to make a screen.

"Okay, raise your right leg so I can pull off your Depends and shorts. Good. Okay, now your left."

"I can't. It won't move. I can't move. Get me out of here."

"Take a deep breath. Just try to relax. There's no rush. Let's try it again."

I get the wet mess off of him, sit him in the passenger seat, throw the makeshift screen over him, and toss the soiled laundry in the trunk.

In three minutes, we're back at his assisted living facility. I pull his wet shorts on him.

"You just need to wear these until we can get to your apartment."

I shower him, pull on fresh Depends and clean shorts, give him the next round of medicines, and settle him into his massive power recliner. Ten-minute appointments, my ass.

I called a friend that night to tell her what had happened. I was exhausted and rattled, and I needed to talk to someone.

SLOW LOSS

"Oh my God, that's hilarious," she says.

"No, it's tragic. There's absolutely nothing funny about what happened today."

"Someday, you're going to find a way to make this funny. I can see you telling this story in one of your storytelling performances. It's great material. Make sure you write it down."

"There will never be anything funny about losing Greg like this. Never. I have to go."

Oh, dear friend, please just listen and witness my suffering. Please, please do not trivialize this profound grief, this slow, slicing loss.

LONELINESS IS AN ORANGE DUST MOP

I visit Greg every day to sort his medications, do his laundry, bring him treats he can swallow—like Italian ice or eggnog—and talk about our worlds. Some days we chat about politics or wildlife activities on the river. On other days, he dozes in his recliner, too tired to talk.

The hallucinations have started again, and the neurologist has upped the medication to minimize their frequency. The medication makes him sleepy.

Yesterday, I told Greg about some friends who are going to California for the winter. Both of their sons are working in San Francisco. They're renting a house near Point Reyes, one of our favorite parks, to see their kids and escape New England.

"Please don't tell me about things like this. I don't want to hear what people are doing. It makes me too sad. It reminds me that I'm just sitting here waiting to die. I didn't feel this way in the summer. The shorter days make me feel depressed."

Like Greg, my days feel empty too. I am waiting for my optimistic self to return. I am waiting to reclaim my curiosity, my sense of adventure, my energy, my belief in possibilities. I'm looking for signs.

I walk. I obsess over the perfect lampshade, convinced a lampshade will make my house feel cozier when it's dark in the winter. I learn the twenty-four things you can do with Dawn liquid detergent besides washing dishes. I think about signing up for a class but never get around to it.

I look out the window and wish the three-foot-tall weeds would magically disappear. Despite my wishes, they stand strong and defiant. The branches of the pine trees blew down in a recent storm, but the weeds stand tall.

"How is he doing?" friends ask about Greg.

"No crises," I say because they don't really want details. When I have explained what's happening with his health, I feel like I'm scaring or boring them, or both.

I wonder why they don't ask how I'm doing. I am so lonely. Lost and purposeless. They probably wouldn't like to hear that. I'm stuck in my New England narrative, "You can do this. The world doesn't want complainers or whiners. Just put one foot in front of the other." People see me as strong, so I must be. "You are the bravest woman we know." Ha. I'm just surviving one day to the next.

Maybe they ask how I'm doing, but I don't hear their kindness. Maybe they don't ask or probe because I don emotional armor, thinking it will protect me from coming undone. I am a slow-loss warrior, determined to survive whatever Greg and his disease throw at me next.

Last night, we had the first deep frost. The radiators clinked awake like a quiet stereophonic symphony, ringing from one side of a room to another.

LONELINESS IS AN ORANGE DUST MOP

I put the winter comforter on the bed, snuggled into its warmth, and opened Pema Chödrön's book, *How We Live Is How We Die*.

"The end of one experience is the beginning of the next experience," she writes, kindly urging us to accept the "truth of reality" and the notion of perpetual impermanence. We are always in transition, something ending and something beginning.

The next morning, I get out the orange dust mop and sweep it under the radiators, moving from room to room. My new-found housekeeping habits are no longer a strident attempt at control. They're more of a relaxing, mindful practice. I find a weird comfort in dusting, mopping, and folding clean clothes. It's meditative and slow. There are no deadlines, no "right" way to do it, and I feel a sense of accomplishment when finished.

Can I take the same slow approach to letting possibilities unfold on their own schedule? Should I put "You Can't Hurry Love" on my playlists to remind myself that I am mourning my husband, though he is still alive, and that I can't rush through it?

A therapist friend reassures me. "You're like Tigger from *Winnie the Pooh*. You've lost your bounces. They'll return, but it takes time. You can't rush through what you're feeling."

I shake out the mop and hear the quiet hum of the refrigerator and the angry sound of leaf blowers in the neighbors' yards. A gardener friend tells me that if it snows before you pick up the oak and maple leaves, your lawn could develop a terrible fungus. Don't wait too long.

I want to extend fall. Winters in New England are dark, cold, and isolating. Up until this past year, spring and summer were my seasons. Everything blooming with new life. If only I could come up with some possibilities, something I'm curious about, something that feels productive and helpful. If only I would commit to friends who ask me to visit.

What am I going to do with myself?

I continue to clean, wondering what might be next. Sorry, Pema. I will read more tonight and try to let go of expectations.

The first snow may fall on Wednesday, on top of my unraked leaves. It will be a dusting if anything. Kind of like the snow that fell in *The Wizard of Oz*, waking Dorothy.

I think of the wise Buddhist nun, Pema Chödrön, as being like Glinda, the Good Witch of the North. She pulls her gnarled and wise eighty-six-year-old hands out of her orange monk's robe, smiles, and suggests another approach to me: "Just relax."

I put away the cleaning supplies and take a deep breath. Just relax.

ST. JOHN BLESSES ME

"I know it's last minute," says our friend Rosanne's email, "but we're planning Wayne's memorial celebration here on the island on what would have been his sixty-ninth birthday. It's going to be one of those celebrations Wayne always liked where people come down for a while and leave with a new friend. Can you come?"

Greg seems stable. Since the trip to the oral surgeon, he has not left the assisted living center. Any change in his routine triggers paranoia and hallucinations. My number one priority is to keep things predictable for him. Should I go?

"You should go to St. John," says Greg. "Here I wrote this about Wayne. Will you read it at the memorial?" The writing is incoherent, but I assure him I will read it.

I talk with the director of nursing and arrange for CNAs to check on him more often while I'm away. I triple-check that his medications are filled and organized properly. I fill his little refrigerator with his favorite Italian ices and yogurt.

SLOW LOSS

"See you in a week."

"Go, go, stop worrying so much. You deserve to have some fun."

Our friends Wayne and Rosanne moved from Rhode Island to St. John in January 2009: Wayne to manage the Concordia eco-resort, and Rosanne to start a property management and architectural firm. They married in late January of that year at the eco-resort.

Greg and I went down for a week to be part of the festivities, staying in one of the platform tents that back up to the U.S. Virgin Islands National Park and overlook Ram's Head Bay. We climbed ninety-three steps to get to the parking lot from our tent and climbed down fifty-six steps to get to the casual restaurant and reception area.

Wayne believed that everyone who came to their wedding should leave with at least one new best friend. Most of the guests, like us, stayed for a week.

We all joined hands as Wayne and Rosanne made their vows by the yoga pavilion. This was no fancy-dancy "destination wedding." We wore beach sandals, Hawaiian shirts, linen caftans, and lots of sunscreen. After eating under the pavilion, we cleared the food, moved tables, and danced to a local band.

Greg had been experiencing headaches and a pinched nerve in his neck for months before this trip. In retrospect, I see that these were symptoms of Parkinson's, which had not yet been diagnosed.

Before Ian started school, Greg and I used to rent a house here in January as a Christmas present for family and friends. People, wet bathing suits, port-a-cribs, and flip-flops packed the house. My mother snorkeled. I swam and read. My father and Greg sat on the beach with their Budweisers. My sisters ran after Ian as he chased

ST. JOHN BLESSES ME

a wild donkey into the mangroves. At the end of the day, we took outdoor showers, cooked dinner, and went to bed early.

The island is not for everyone. Wild donkeys, goats, and lizards walk the roads and beaches. Mice run wild in kitchens if you don't store everything in the refrigerator. The driving is treacherous, with mountain switchbacks and disorienting left-hand side driving. There are no resorts, fancy restaurants, or beachfront cabanas with refreshments. Internet connection can be sporadic, as can electricity. Solar heats the water in many houses and campsites. If it's cloudy, you're taking a cold shower.

The trip to St. John for Wayne and Rosanne's wedding was the last big trip Greg and I took.

The afternoon after Wayne's memorial celebration, about twenty-five of us board three boats at the tiny marina behind the infamous Skinny Legs bar and head out to a secluded cove near the east end of the island. We tie the boats together and anchor for what locals call "a raft-up." Some older people get comfortable under the awning on one of the boats. Most of us wrap swimming noodles under our arms, grab a drink in a plastic cup, and hang out in the water.

I bob and chat with one or two people, and then I paddle over to another group. We tell stories about Wayne. We chat about the octopus someone had seen while snorkeling. I talk with Rosanne about her grief and about what is going on in her head and heart. She asks me about Greg.

Someone starts doing water acrobatics. We laugh and learn she has won national competitions and competed in the Olympics. We goad her into performing. Twenty of us form a large circle in the water, and Kate performs in the middle. She dives under the water, and then her two legs appear straight up, and then she does scissor kicks.

I don't know if it was the alcohol or the deep sense of love that infected us, but by the end of the afternoon, some of us decide we should go down the slide on one of the boats.

"I don't know," I say.

"Lois, we have to do it," says my new friend, Kevin, twenty-seven years younger than me. "What do you think, Natalie? Are you in? Lois and I are going to do it."

For the next hour, we climb up the ladder, fly off the slide into the water, come up for air, laugh, and squeal, "Again!"

As we headed back into the marina, we talked about this day and how it was the best day ever—what some might call collective effervescence.

Now, it's time to head home. The eleven fifteen ferry from St. John to Charlotte Amalie waits for its passengers. Its sister ferry to Red Hook is sleek, modern, spacious, without rust, and with ample seating above and below deck. This one is a clunker. Sometimes it's working, and sometimes it's out of commission for a month or more.

Just ten of us board the eleven fifteen, all but one person sit on the sturdy benches at the open stern of the boat. It is a balmy eighty-five degrees, breezy and humid with ominous clouds.

The sun peeks out as the ferry workers toss our luggage onto the open deck, a neat heap of roller bags, duffel bags, and oversized backpacks. They pull the lines up from the dock. The ferry horn gives a low blast, and we move away.

ST. JOHN BLESSES ME

A family of four looks exhausted. They are sunburned, wear wrinkled black travel clothes, and have stern faces, like they've had too much vacation together. A middle-aged couple my age looks at the sky. She's dressed in a silky black-and-white halter dress and gold leather Gladiator sandals. Her brown bob looks like she just walked out of a salon. How is she defying this humidity?

She goes below. Her husband looks at me and shrugs his shoulders. He wears ferry-appropriate clothes: nylon shorts, a T-shirt, and sneakers, much like me.

I put my face to the sun and take in the warmth. Thank you, thank you, God, for the return of joy this past week despite being here for a friend's memorial celebration. I want to store up these feelings as I head back to the dark, coldness of New England, back to my husband.

The ferry moves past the lush hills of the tiny islands between St. John and St. Thomas. So green, so wild.

The butterfly bloom this week has been especially magical. It is the first in six years, the first since the devastating 2017 hurricanes—Irma and Maria. All week the yellow, white, and orange butterflies swarmed around me as I drove my jeep down rutted, dirt roads to my favorite beaches and sat on my porch listening to the baby goat crying on the rocky beach below the house.

"Hello, my fairies, or are you my guardian angels?" They dip and rise and playfully fly off together, loving their island, loving the return of the ecosystem after such destruction. We are back. Woosh.

"Goodbye, my angels," I say as the ferry moves away from the islands.

The wind gusts. Rain sprinkles, but it's a soft rain. Half the people go below deck. I pull my raincoat out of my pack and zip it up. Mr. Appropriately Dressed gives me a thumbs up. He has no raingear.

The boat hits a swell and water sprays the deck, soaking us. Everyone goes below deck but me.

The rain turns fierce, stinging my face. It is an angry rain, daring me. "Will you choose the safe way or stay in the mess of life, with all its tragic and beautiful surprises?"

The ferry worker throws a tarp over the luggage. I put my feet on it, so it won't blow away. He gestures for me to go below. I shake my head no. He not only goes below but also closes and locks the heavy steel door, keeping the rain and ocean swells from seeping into the cabin.

"Thank you, thank you God or guardian angels or Mother Nature. Thank you for this, I pray as I sit in the storm, feeling more alive than I have in years.

The wind shifts, still strong but from a different direction, like a protective power is waking me up, encouraging me to pay attention. To feel it all.

As the ferry gets closer to the harbor, the storm moves off to the north. I take off my REI raincoat, which has flunked its waterproof claims. My wet shorts and T-shirt stick to my body. Water drips from my hair into my eyes.

The sun comes out.

The steel door opens, and people emerge from the protected cabin, dry, serious, intently looking for their luggage and hoping it's dry.

They look up at me, alone and soaked. I smile.

Oh, the joy and freedom from staying in the storm. I'm alive. Truly alive. There's more. Much more of life left for me.

DURING: 2023

THE WALL OF PICTURES

"Can you believe those guys are taking down the pilings in the river? Look at them with their shirts off. It's Thanksgiving, right? Why would they be working today and not with any clothes on?"

I walk over to the windows and take a look.

"Um, honey. I don't think there are any men out there."

"Of course there are. They've been working on the river pilings every day."

Greg's hallucinations are becoming more frequent. Some of the hallucinations frighten him. Some days, he can't tell the difference between what is real and what is a hallucination. He takes Seroquel to manage the hallucinations and other psychotic symptoms, but he's pretty maxed out on how much of this drug he can safely take.

The neurologist explains the hallucinations are from both the disease *and* years of taking so much carbidopa-levodopa medicine. People who have taken carbidopa levodopa and then were diagnosed with a disease other than Parkinson's were far less likely to hallucinate.

"By the way, I like that you sleep on the floor next to my bed," says Greg. "When you were in St. John, you slept on my floor every night."

"What?"

"I know you weren't really here. I know I was hallucinating. Some hallucinations are good, you know."

After we agree no men are working on the river, and that they are hallucinations, we drink a glass of champagne. It is Thanksgiving Day.

I asked Greg if he wanted to come home for Thanksgiving, but he said no. He doesn't even want to go for a ride. It has become too much for him to leave this place, physically and cognitively. He craves predictability and familiarity.

After so much change this year, this holiday feels OK. Greg feels safe, and I feel relieved. Neither of us is upset that it isn't Thanksgiving as usual.

Greg has been in assisted living for six months. He is twelve years into the disease.

We are adjusting, letting go of what once was. But on this favorite holiday, I am sad. Greg is more accepting of the realities. He's not fighting anymore. He has stopped saying I am the cause of his illness and the disturbing symptoms like paranoia and delusions. He acknowledges that his disease is winning. He reminds me: "Please, whatever happens, no hospitals. Don't do that to me. Let me go quietly."

Greg's obsessions and impulse behavior continue. A new one is printing and framing photos of his life. He sends photos to CVS to be printed, framed, and mailed to him.

He has hung almost a hundred pictures along a big wall of his apartment. There are photos and picture frames stacked on each of the six windowsills, waiting to be hung. When I open the kitchen cabinets, there are picture frames. When I open the hall closet, there are picture frames. There are holes in the wall where he hammered

THE WALL OF PICTURES

picture hangers and then yanked them out. He spends hours every day adding to and rearranging his picture wall.

"I love to sit in my recliner and look at the wall," he reflects. "I've done so much in my life. People here can't believe what I've done. I bring them here and show them."

The pictures near the top of the wall show mountain activities, while the ones at the bottom are ocean-related.

"That's Ian up on top of the wall hiking Mount Katahdin, us hiking on the Isle of Skye, and me and Russ rock climbing in Wales.

"Do you see the one down there with me wearing #246 on my running shorts? That was from the road race on Block Island, where we met. There's a picture of us at your prom.

"Greg Jr.'s pictures are lower on the wall because he lives on the water. Pictures of our dogs are next to Greg because he's a vet.

"The whole lower right section is pictures from our pond. The swans, the geese, the blue herons, and lots of sunsets and parties.

"When you step back and look at the whole wall, it looks like a giant fish. Do you see the patterns?"

"I do."

"It's a work in progress," he says. "The patterns keep changing. The CNAs love coming in here and seeing the wall. They can't believe how much I've done in my life. There's a picture of you in Skye. See it?"

"Scotland was a great trip except for that hike. I see a lot of pictures of your dogs. I can't believe there are so many of Mookie. That dog was a terror, a killer. Why did I let you keep him? Why didn't I insist he be put down?"

"That was a mistake. I should have put him down sooner, but I loved that dog so much. It's hard to give up creatures you love."

There are so many questions about a long marriage that we can't answer, yet we're trying to have these conversations as he declines.

SLOW LOSS

"What did you like about being married?" I ask.

"I need to think about that. Whoa. Do you see the person behind me throwing darts at my wall? Why would anyone throw darts at my wall?"

"Greg, there's no person throwing darts at the wall."

"There isn't? That's a relief. Now, back to your question. I liked that we were both different and took risks. That we didn't fit any traditional norms. I liked that I did what I wanted, and you did what you wanted."

"Yes. But I feel like we grew apart when we each did what we wanted. I wish we found more things that we liked to do together."

"Probably," he says. "But overall, we had a good life."

"Yes. I especially loved your kindness and thoughtfulness."

This conversation is exhausting Greg. His voice starts to slur, and his dyskinesia worsens. We sip our champagne and look at the wall. Looking at the wall comforts him.

Last winter, we knew things were getting worse, but we could never have imagined how quickly he would deteriorate in just six months. After years of slow and small changes, we didn't expect such a steep, fast decline. We didn't know that the disease could be so sneaky and unpredictable. We thought there was more time. We never imagined the violence, the psych wards, the relentless hallucinations.

A year ago, Greg said the only way he would ever leave his home would be in a coffin. It turned out to be a stretcher and straitjacket six months later.

He's getting tired, and I need to leave and have a quiet Thanksgiving dinner with Greg's brother and his wife at a local restaurant. No twenty-pound turkeys. Tables for twenty. Coolers on the deck filled with beer, wine, and champagne. Bossy-pants sisters taking over my kitchen. Countertops filled with leftovers and mounds of dishes to be cleaned over several dishwasher cycles.

THE WALL OF PICTURES

"I love my picture wall. I love seeing my life. I'll try to find a way to put some more pictures of you on the wall. Go and have a good Thanksgiving dinner."

I am so grateful I can leave, that I can go home tonight to quiet, that the denials about the disease and accusations aimed at me are gone.

I am so thankful his wall comforts Greg and reminds him of how fully he lived his life.

I AM FALLING APART, THANK YOU FOR ASKING

Greg is quickly falling apart, and I am powerless.

I don't want to write about things falling apart. I am a fixer. Corporate crises. Children's injuries. Dying dogs. Assisted living arrangements for a fiercely independent husband. Check, check, check, check. Yet, I may be losing my talents.

This morning, I called Greg, and he said he was OK. He had breakfast with some of his men friends and plans to take a nap. Ah, a morning to myself. No rushing. No busyness.

I sit quietly and drink coffee from my cheery polka-dot mug. I look out the window and watch a blue heron standing in the pond.

The heron turns its head, and I think she's sending me a message, "Things are under control. Things are not falling apart." It's what I want to hear. I love this beautiful creature.

Then all eighteen of the smoke alarms in the house start blaring. Not the "chirp, chirp, chirp" of low batteries but an ominous, BLEEP, BLEEP, BLEEP.

SLOW LOSS

I put down the mug and run from room to room to find the danger. Garage? Nothing. Kitchen? OK. Guest room? Fine.

"BLEEP, BLEEP, BLEEP. Warning! Warning!"

I run downstairs and open the door to the furnace room. No fires. Has that oil smell always been there?

I'm about to run down the hall to check on the other rooms when the alarms stop. All of them. From cacophony to silence. From fear and warning to relief and bewilderment. What the hell was that?

This house, I'm sure, is haunted, sending me messages I can't decipher.

I've owned homes for forty years and know what can go wrong. I know how to fix common problems, or at least who to call.

But living in this house I never wanted over the past two years reminds me that I'm falling apart, out of control. Or is it that I have no control?

I want to fix my loneliness, but I have no energy to invite people over for dinner, go to an ecstatic dance class, or even call a friend. It's easier to just sit here drinking my coffee.

I want to fix my husband's suffering and help him enjoy what he can. I'm uncomfortable with his increasingly frequent musings about when he's going to die and whether there's anything we can do to speed up the process.

Some days I'm calm and sit and listen to his frustrations, sadness, and worries about how the end might be.

"I don't want to be in the nursing home with a feeding tube. I don't want people to have to change my diapers and wipe drool from my mouth. Is that what's going to happen? There's got to be a way out."

On other days I'm not calm and patient. My fixer personality goes wild. I urge him to get involved in activities at the assisted living community, nag him about not eating solid foods because he'll

I AM FALLING APART, THANK YOU FOR ASKING

choke, and obsessively clean his apartment. This is not helpful to him. Why can't I stop and just sit quietly with him? Read while he naps. Eat ice cream together. I will try harder.

Every year, my friend Maria and I choose a word to be our guiding star. I chose UNWIND for this year because I thought it meant unwinding from the 24/7 stress of taking care of Greg now that he's in assisted living.

But my unwinding has taken on a different meaning: falling apart.

Who am I without my husband, work, dreams of adventure, the ability to impulsively go to New York or wherever? Who am I living in this unpredictable house that I didn't want to buy? Who am I unable to commit to plans?

I try to flip my thinking. What good surprises might come from letting go of control? Of letting old attachments and behaviors fall away? Who might I become?

When sisters, cousins, friends, and neighbors ask how I am, maybe I will tell them I am falling apart.

"Oh no," they'll say and offer fixes or platitudes.

I'll cut them off and tell them that I am transforming from a fixer to a whirling dervish, spinning, swirling in a gold chiffon skirt, dancing to my soul's silent music, shaking off fear.

I am falling apart, and I am fine, thank you for asking.

THE DYING MANATEE

"Lois, I'm calling you before they do. Everything is OK, but I had to call 911," says Greg.

"Did you faint again? Did you fall?" Greg's blood pressure drops very low in the mornings, usually at breakfast, and he has been fainting three or four times a week. The assisted living center calls me whenever this happens.

"No, I'm fine. I looked out my window and saw hundreds of dead manatees along the side of the river. I walked across the street to see them up close. They weren't dead, but they were dying, so I called 911.

"The fire engine and ambulance came and wanted to know where I live. They took me back to The Tock and told me there were no manatees, only rocks. I really am losing it."

Three days later, Greg is upset again by lifelike hallucinations.

"How was your night?" I ask him as I gather dirty towels and clothes to do his laundry.

"My entire Matta extended family was outside standing on the sidewalk last night. There must have been a hundred of them. Aunts, uncles, cousins. I tried to get out of the building to talk to them, but the doors were locked. I came back up to the apartment and looked out the windows, and they were still there, looking up at me. They wouldn't leave. Someone would step forward, say something to me, and then disappear. Could this have happened? It felt so real. I was so upset. I think they said mean things to me."

"Oh, Greg, it sounds like a bad hallucination."

"They're getting much worse."

"I'm so sorry you're going through this. You know your Portuguese aunts and cousins would never say mean things to you."

"I hope not."

There are symptoms more troubling than hallucinations and fainting. Greg isn't eating much, sleeps most of the day, and has lost interest in listening to books.

Though Greg has been an introvert most of his life, he's enjoyed eating at the "guys' breakfast table" and getting to know the other men living at the assisted living center. "Even though they're much older than me, we have a lot of interests in common." Greg's friends are in their late eighties and nineties. He is seventy-four.

He has also stopped going to the dining room to see his friends for breakfast.

Something is wrong.

The nurse practitioner thinks it might be a urinary tract infection or COVID. They do blood work. Everything looks normal.

I call the neurologist who has overseen Greg's PD since the beginning. He is on a sabbatical. The covering neurologist suggests a new medication called Nuplazid to help with hallucinations. The cost for a thirty-day supply is $5,200, and it will likely take up to six weeks for symptoms to ease. It has an efficacy rate of 13.7 percent. Are you kidding me? Five thousand dollars and a 14 percent chance that it will work? I say no to this drug and ask what else we might try. We are out of new things to try.

The director of nursing reassures me that this might just be a virus and may resolve itself.

I stay with Greg all day and into the evenings, going home to sleep and shower. When he screams in his sleep, I hold his hand and reassure him he's safe. I make him protein shakes and let him binge on as many Pepperidge Farm Goldfish as he can eat without choking.

One Saturday morning I walk into Greg's apartment, and it is trashed. Pictures have been taken off the wall. Soiled Depends are strewn around the room. A chair is overturned. Gatorade is spilled on the rugs in the bedroom and living room.

Greg is lying on his bed, naked. The sheets and blankets are in a heap on the floor.

I cannot wake Greg, though he is breathing.

I pull the emergency call button.

"Yes?"

"Something is wrong with my husband. I need a nurse right away."

"It's Saturday, no nurses are working in assisted living."

I march down to the main desk. "I need a nurse right now. There must be a nurse in the memory care or skilled nursing units who can see my husband. This is urgent."

"Would you like me to call an ambulance?"

"No, I would like you to call a nurse."

I go back to Greg's apartment, clean him up, put on a new Depends, and cover him with a sheet and blankets, which he promptly kicks off.

"Greg, can you hear me? Greg?"

Nothing.

A nurse comes from the memory care unit, takes Greg's blood pressure, examines his skin, and sees him punch the air with one of his arms and try to kick off the sheet again.

SLOW LOSS

"I think your husband has terminal agitation. I think he may be dying."

"What do I do? He doesn't want to go to a hospital."

"Call hospice and see if they can get over here today. He needs someone with him at all times. Don't leave his side."

Hospice can't come until Monday. It is Saturday afternoon. How are we going to make it until Monday morning?

I give Greg extra doses of Seroquel for hallucinations and two Ativan to try to calm the agitation. I call my sister, a nurse practitioner, for advice.

"He's calm, but what if I gave him too much medication?"

She reassures me that I did the right thing.

"You want to keep him as comfortable as you can. You did the right thing not sending Greg to the hospital. You're doing what he wants."

There are four things I remember about this weekend, the longest weekend in my life: Rosie, fire alarms, Goldfish, and Frankenstein.

"Hi, I'm Greg's wife. Could I get some yogurt and ginger ale?" I ask a dining room attendant at Greg's facility.

"You are Greg's wife? How is my Greg doing?" she asks.

"He's having a hard time."

"Your Greg, he is such a good man. My name is Rosie. He asked me if I was named for Rosie the Riveter. I don't know Rosie the Riveter, and he tells me the story. And then he buys me a poster of Rosie the Riveter. I have it in my living room. Yes, your Greg, a good, good man."

On Saturday night—or was it the early hours of Sunday— the fire alarms go off in the building, and "evacuate, evacuate" blares from the speakers. (What is it with me and these fire alarms?) One, two, seven fire trucks pull up in front of the building, red lights swirling like a disco scene.

Greg is medicated and asleep. It would take two skilled people to get him into a wheelchair and wheel him outside. Too tired to panic, I figure someone will come and evacuate us if the situation is serious. None of the alarms wake Greg.

I watch the fire trucks from the window and wonder what the problem could be. I wonder if Greg is dying as the nurse suggested or whether this is just another decline. Though he's had the disease for twelve years, my friends' husbands have been living with PD for much longer.

The "evacuate, evacuate" voice alarm stops. The honking alarm continues.

Firefighters leave the building, pack up hoses and axes, and one, two, and seven fire trucks leave.

I go to the registration desk to ask someone when the honking alarm will go off. It's starting to feel like noise torture. Like I'm a prisoner of war. I cannot find anyone. I go back upstairs, check on Greg, and sit in his blue recliner, waiting for morning, waiting for the alarm to stop.

By Sunday night, I'm exhausted. I get Greg to drink some water and take his meds, but he seems unaware of what's going on and is nonverbal. I call the hospice to confirm the Monday morning evaluation appointment, and I eat the yogurts and ice cream in the refrigerator.

I take half of one of Greg's Ativan for myself and lay down in the recliner. What harm can a little antianxiety medicine do?

I wake up startled. Greg is yelling at me.

"Hey, hey, hey, you're supposed to be taking care of me," he says, standing in front of the recliner. All the apartment lights are on. The refrigerator door is open, as are the kitchen cabinet doors.

What have I slept through? Oh my gosh, Greg is awake and mobile? I am so irresponsible. How could I have fallen asleep? This is not the time to medicate myself.

Greg puts his hand into a giant, four-pound box of Goldfish, grabs a handful of the crackers, and stuffs them into his mouth. Half of them land on the floor.

"Since you're awake, how about taking some of your meds?"

"Don't tell me what to do," he says, rocking from one foot to the other. "I can do what I want."

He's upright without his rollator, eating and talking. So, probably not dying.

He doesn't want to talk to me. Greg eats the Goldfish and looks out the windows to the river. "Are the guys out there working on the barge? I think I see them."

The sky is getting lighter. I give Greg his PD meds, but not the Ativan because I want him alert when the hospice nurse arrives at 8:00 a.m.

"Greg, on a scale of one to ten, what's your pain level," the hospice nurse asks as part of the evaluation.

"Probably just a two. I feel good."

Greg is alert and engaged in conversation with the nurse.

Greg raises his legs and arms when asked, squeezes the nurse's hand, answers cognitive questions accurately, and suggests that the nurse take a look at The Wall of Pictures.

"I remember everything," Greg says. "There's nothing wrong with my mind."

The nurse says he'll consult with the admitting physician and get back to me.

Within three hours, Greg has fallen back to an unresponsive yet agitated state.

"What do I do?" I ask the assisted living director of nursing. "What if hospice doesn't admit Greg? He was like his old normal self during the evaluation. Do I find a skilled nursing facility? Should I send him to the hospital? What should I be thinking about?"

"Let's see what hospice says."

"Do you know anyone at hospice? Didn't you say you worked for them a while back? Can you call over and tell them what's been happening during the past three weeks with Greg? I think that nurse this morning thought I was overreacting. What he saw is not how Greg has been. I need you to do something. Please, call in favors if you can."

During Greg's stay here for the past ten months, I've bent over backward to be nice and pleasant to everyone involved in his care. But not today. It's clear that if I don't demand what I need, nothing is likely to happen. A helpful CNA tells me that it's time to be a squeaky wheel.

The director of nursing assures me she'll make some calls. She does, and she comes to Greg's apartment to check on him. His blood pressure has dropped. He seems to be having violent dreams.

At 5:00 p.m. another nurse from hospice arrives.

"I want Greg to be comfortable. I can see he's suffering and agitated. This has been going on for weeks. Please help me get him into hospice care."

After many forms and calls with the hospice physician, the nurse tells me that an ambulance is scheduled. Greg will be admitted tonight.

I am so relieved. We have a plan of some sort.

Between the time the hospice nurse leaves, and the ambulance arrives, Greg rises from his bed like Frankenstein. He walks into the walls. Pushes me when I try to get him back into the bed. Falls sideways holding on to his rollator and gashes his leg.

A CNA comes to help me get Greg off the floor and back into bed. Her pager keeps buzzing.

"Sorry, I have to leave, but I'll be back to check on him."

Greg gets out of bed again. Pushes me hard as I try to get him back to bed. He falls again.

"Would you stop it?" I scream. "Why are you doing this? Please, please, please get into bed or just sit. Stop fighting me." He pushes me out of his way; he is still so strong.

I call for the CNA again and plead for her to stay with us until the ambulance arrives. She has a friendly, no-nonsense style that calms Greg and me down. She makes small talk to Greg, reminds him that "he better stop fooling around" because she's bigger and stronger than him.

THE DYING MANATEE

The ambulance drivers arrive on time, settle Greg into a gurney and remark about The Wall of Pictures.

"They're pictures of my life. I did so much. And there are hidden pictures of penises and vaginas. Want to see them?"

Cogent and crazy.

"Where are my phone and iPad? I need them now, Lois. Now."

"Greg, I'll bring them. Don't worry. I'm going to follow the ambulance and will be with you."

The hospice staff quickly get Greg settled into a room and give him some medication to ease his agitation. They tell me that there's nothing more I can do for now.

I go home at midnight to shower and sleep in my own bed.

EVERYTHING IS IN ORDER AND OTHER LIES

I take the last sip of milky coffee and look out the kitchen window. The rising sun hits the treetops across the pond.

The geese stand by the edge of the pond, trying to figure out how to get by the homemade fence I built. Oh no, you won't. No crapping all over my yard.

I wash the white porcelain Hario coffee dripper and put it on the drying rack. Next, I wash my favorite Polish Pottery bubble mug. Muted blue tulips are painted on the mug, blooming from the mug's round base. I squirt a little more Dawn detergent in the mug and scrub the insides with a clean, yellow sponge. Instead of putting it on the drying rack, I dry it with a frayed linen dish towel.

I am procrastinating. I need to go to the hospice.

It's 5:50 a.m. Should I have stayed last night? But I was so exhausted from sleeping on his floor for the past five nights, alert, on-call, and anxious. Will Greg be angry that I didn't stay?

I put the tulip bubble mug back on its shelf next to the Sumatra coffee. I need to go.

I need to text our sons. Should I have done that last night? No, I would have woken them. And I would have had to talk to them.

There are no words left. But I must.

"Dad was admitted to the hospice center last night. On my way there now. Will call when I know more."

But I don't leave.

I slide open the kitchen door and run down the deck stairs and across the yard. I run fast, wave my arms, and scream at the geese. "Get out of my yard you fuckers. Shoo. Scram. Get lost. Shit somewhere else."

The geese flap their wings in disdain. Who is this madwoman? We're just easing into the morning, eating grass and relieving ourselves. Calm down, lady.

I throw a rock at them. They lift off, fly halfway across the pond, and land in the water, honking with annoyance.

I walk back up the stairs, take off my muddy clogs, and wipe the kitchen counters. Everything is in order. And everything is out of control.

I open the garage door, put Greg's phone and charger on the passenger seat, and back out of the driveway.

The text messages are pinging. "Driving can't talk. Will call."

I have to get Greg's phone and iPad to him.

I have to talk to the hospice doctor. Is Greg really dying? Or is this a false alarm? Another quirky PD agitation symptom?

I have to call our sons, his brother, my sisters.

I have to remember to eat.

I have to buy more coffee.

I have to figure out a backup plan if he's discharged.

I have to not feel shame about hoping that this is the end.

I have to find my sunglasses and put the visor down. I can't see where I'm going.

MY BIG FAT PORTUGUESE DEATH VIGIL

When I arrive at the hospice, Greg is unconscious and calmer, though still trying to rip out the IV and take off his johnny.

"Are you OK with us giving him more medication to relieve the agitation?" asks the doctor. "This means he's unlikely to regain consciousness."

"Yes, anything to stop the suffering."

"Could you just step out of the room for a few minutes while we get him comfortable?"

When I walk into the hall, I see Greg's brother talking to some of the Matta cousins—cousins who had been in Greg's hallucination.

"How did you know Greg was here already," I ask.

"We didn't. Our mother is across the hall."

"Aunt Irene is dying, and she's across the hall?"

"Yes. She came in five days ago. Can you believe it? What are the odds of two Mattas dying at the same time and being across the hall from one another?"

SLOW LOSS

And so began a week of My Big Fat Portuguese Death Vigil.

My Boston family deals with dying with as few people around as possible. The immediate family and the person dying. We keep things quiet. We talk little, dispense medications, clean the house, hold our mother/father's hand, make sure we've got food in the kitchen, and call the rest of the relatives when it's all over. Talking takes too much emotional energy. Visitors are not welcome.

"Please, we're OK. We'll need you when this is over but not now."

I thought this was how it would go with my husband. A quiet hospice center, our sons and his brother sitting with me until he passed.

Greg's hallucination of the one hundred Matta relatives was like one of those ghostly premonitions in a Shakespeare play. Here they all were at the hospice center. And no one was disappearing into the ether.

My first reaction was, "How am I going to deal with all these people? How can I be social and chatty when my husband is dying? Should I have brought him home to die instead of going to a hospice center? When I'm exhausted, I sometimes say snarky things. Do I have any brain cells left to keep my mouth shut if I get irritated or if my bitchy dark side rises like Persephone, the Queen of the Underworld? Please, God, don't let me say anything I'll regret."

That's the last logical train of thought I had. I just stopped thinking. I was too exhausted to be anxious about what I might do or say. The disease had worn me down. I was out of gas. I turned the lights off in Greg's room and sat with him. Whatever was going to happen was going to happen.

After a few hours of sitting alone with my husband, there was a quiet knock on the door.

MY BIG FAT PORTUGUESE DEATH VIGIL

"Hey, Lois, we're going upstairs to the cafeteria for a cup of tea. Want to take a break and join us?"

Two of Aunt Irene's daughters and I drank our tea in the small cafeteria. The conversation was slow and effortless. We were all out of emotional gas. Though I've known them for forty years, I feel a new closeness, a shared vulnerability. We're walking in the dark together.

"So, what are you thinking about arrangements?" someone asks.

"I don't know. Maybe Greg's mother's Congregational Church or maybe Our Lady of Fatima. I felt so depressed last Christmas that I went to Fatima by myself. I loved that church. I had never been there before."

"You know the story, right?"

"Um, no."

"Our grandfather—and Greg's—owned the land that the church is built on. He sold the land to the archdiocese and then donated money to build the church and the bell tower. Each bell is engraved with the name of one of the Mattas. How funny you ended up there and didn't know the family story."

We share ideas on which funeral home, cemetery, and florist to choose; where to have the postservice lunch; and where to post the obituaries. I feel so grateful. I hadn't given any thought to what to do, but now these logistical decisions feel easier.

We gravitate back to the rooms where we sit, keeping our individual and collective vigils.

Cousins arrive after work, visiting one relative and then another. Greg Jr. arrives from Miami.

I go home and sleep like the dead, knowing people who love Greg are with him tonight.

"I stayed and talked to Greg until ten," one of his cousins tells me the next day.

This cousin is known as the family talker and storyteller. He is a compassionate, big-hearted guy. When Greg moved into the assisted living facility last summer, this cousin asked if he could visit. "Yes," said Greg. "But tell him no more than an hour. You know how he can talk."

"When I was with Greg last night, I think he said something to me. It was hard to hear him, but I put my face close to his and he said it again. I think he said, "Shut up."

I burst out laughing. My husband's last words were honest as always.

I regale the other Matta cousins with the story.

"Shut up? That is priceless."

The death vigil is getting loud and social.

My bossy bitchiness starts to melt in the hospice center.

I dab a damp sponge on my husband's dry lips. Though unconscious, he moves his lips like a bass fish, desperate for water. I dip the sponge in a cup of water and give him more.

He is safe. The hospice staff gives him pain medication, changes his johnny and catheter, gives him tender sponge baths, trims his beard, changes his sheets, and dims the lights.

These are no longer my responsibilities. Nor do I have to manage the neurologist, cardiologist, urologist, primary care physician, assisted living aides, thirty-eight different daily pills, his laundry, porn addiction, obsessive spending, and the fallout from the lifelike nasty hallucinations.

MY BIG FAT PORTUGUESE DEATH VIGIL

We have safely made it to the end.

The light in his room is soft. I hold his hand. There is nothing else I have to do. No other place I need to be. Just here.

My phone blows up with loving texts. "What can we do? What do you need?"

I have no energy to respond.

"What can I do? Do you want something to eat from the cafeteria?" asks Greg Jr. "Do you want me to call Clara? Do you think I should come back to the hospice after dinner?"

I hold up my hand. "Please, you decide. I'm not making any more decisions."

I finally answer text messages. "Do whatever you think is best."

Someone else asks. "Should we get pizza? Should we have cots set up so you can sleep here? Do you think he needs more pain medication?'

"You decide. Remember, I'm not making any decisions."

As my husband dies, so does my need to be a bossy bitch.

I'm done.

My husband's cousin, whose mother is dying across the hall, says the kindest thing to me.

"When this is all over, you should do whatever you want."

When we're alone, I tell Greg I won't have the service at a Catholic Church. The nuns at his parochial school repeatedly told him that his mother was going to hell because she was a Protestant. He hated the Catholic church as much as he loved his mother.

"Aunt Irene's service will be at Our Lady of Fatima, but we'll go to the chapel. It seems right. It was your mother's church, and both Greg Jr. and Ian were baptized there."

SLOW LOSS

Greg squeezes my hand hard in acknowledgment, so hard that my wedding ring crushes my finger. This worries me and I go to the nurses' station to find the doctor.

"My husband is still so strong. Are you sure that he's dying?"

"He really is dying," she says so kindly.

On Saturday, five days into the Portuguese Death Vigil, everyone is here, bouncing between rooms.

Greg's sister's son, a minister from Connecticut whom I've asked to do the service, arrives with his four children. "Dying is part of life," he tells his children in Greg's room. "It's very sad but not something to be afraid of."

A cousin brings a flowering spring plant into Greg's room. "We need to have some beauty here," she knowingly says.

An aunt arrives with her rosary beads and does a prayer ritual. She holds Greg's hand, kisses his head, and takes a deep breath. "Greg and I were never close. But we were never far apart. Do you get what I mean?"

I do. So many relationships are like that.

"Now I have to go across the hall and see my poor sister."

Someone brings in their sweet, gentle puppy.

"A Portuguese Water Dog!" the cousins gush. "So adorable."

"No, it's a Hungarian Water Dog."

"No way."

They choose to believe that any creature so intelligent and well-behaved must be Portuguese.

MY BIG FAT PORTUGUESE DEATH VIGIL

Sunday night gets quiet.

Different groups of relatives get together and make dinner plans.

"Want to come with us?"

"No, I'm going to stay here. I'll get some mac and cheese at the cafeteria."

Irene's youngest daughter, who had been the lead caregiver for her ninety-six-year-old mother, hangs back too. Our Spidey senses know that The Big Fat Portuguese Death Vigil is coming to an end. That and the increased morphine that the doctor is giving to these dying Mattas.

"Go home, Brenda. It probably won't be tonight."

"I don't know."

"I'm telling you. Get some sleep. I'll be around for a while and will check in on Irene."

She reluctantly goes home.

Greg Jr. leaves Monday morning after being with me—and all of the Mattas—for most of the week. Ian is due to arrive from Los Angeles in the afternoon.

I close the door to Greg's room. I want my husband all to myself.

When I open the door several hours later, there is a ceramic heart dangling from the door handle.

"I thought you might need that today," says one of Irene's daughters.

Greg's breathing is changing. He looks so handsome and peaceful that I want to take a picture. I want to remember this peaceful version of him, not the hallucinations and agitation, the furrowed brow from so much pain and discomfort, and the mottled, cracked skin from taking so many medications for so many years.

SLOW LOSS

I see Brenda getting ready to leave for the day. I go into the hall to say goodbye.

"I don't know what I'm going to do if I get here tomorrow and you're not here," she says.

We hug. We know.

Greg died at ten thirty that night. Irene died the next night.

There is no right way to do dying. Quiet and intimate like my Boston family. Big and boisterous like my husband's Portuguese família. The only thing I'm sure of is that it's OK to let go of control. To trust in love. To let the hard edges of being a long-haul caregiver shatter.

This was the perfect ending for Greg. His sons, brother, and Portuguese family members from the hallucination were there to hold his hand, speak their love, and reverently say goodbye.

AFTER: 2023–2024

THE LOST SUMMER

Everyone leaves. The last frenetic activity of planning a funeral service and graciously getting through it is over.

My sister, brothers, and brother-in-law have emptied Greg's assisted living apartment. I asked them to figure out what should be donated, tossed, or saved—to make it all go away. They bring just three bins of framed photos from The Picture Wall and a lamp to my house.

People call and text to check in. I have no energy to respond, as well-meaning as they may be. I let everything go unanswered. Is this impolite? Who cares? I can't do a thing. I am exhausted.

I eat the frozen foods people have sent. One day, I eat apple pie for lunch and dinner. Then again, three days in a row.

There's deep relief that the PD odyssey is over. For Greg, for me, for our marriage. Will I ever remember the before days when we danced, hiked, created our dream home bit by bit, and sat in Greg Jr.'s pool in Miami while he and Ian jumped off the house roof into the water?

"Be careful," Greg and I had screamed, so happy for this family, for these kind, intelligent men in our lives, for good times despite the looming knowledge that there was no cure for his PD.

"I bet you sell your house and buy a little cottage in Newport," a neighbor says during my lost summer.

"I am not doing anything. No more big changes."

I sleep and make a feeble attempt to weed and plant some flowers in pots. Though I'm a voracious reader, I have no interest in reading. It takes too much energy.

And then a switch flips.

I default to my comfort zone. I become obsessively busy.

Busyness is my tactic for avoiding difficult, painful emotions. It's one of my superpowers, taught to me by my late mother. No matter what was happening, she would remind me: "We can do this. Let's get things done."

I sort Greg's complicated financial accounts, donate his clothes, trade in his phone and five iPads, auction off his wine, dump the thousands of pennies and nickels he collected into the coin machine at the supermarket, work with the estate attorney to close his estate and update my will, change the registration and title of the damn car, and sort through a lifetime of his photos.

I have not wept over his death. My "to-do" list is my armor against feeling any emotions.

What else can be done?

I sell the house on the pond, sell or donate most of our furniture and household goods, and move into an apartment in the city. I get rid of everything except Greg's voice messages on my phone.

I research psychedelic therapy for grief and trauma and contact a respected Irish psychedelic therapy group to see if I can take part in one of their programs, the sooner the better.

I don't know how to stop, but I do know that I can't keep this pace up. It's probably unhealthy to suppress my emotions. All that energy is likely to explode in a destructive way if left to fester. I've seen this happen to friends. Their repressed feelings erupted in bitterness or self-medication with alcohol.

I want to thaw my stoic, ice-maiden persona, which is often mistaken as bravery or strength. I want to overcome guilt that I could have been a more compassionate wife and caregiver, especially during the last four years of Greg's disease. I want to release whatever emotional constipation is preventing me from sleeping at night. I am so tired.

In my last busyness sprint, I make travel reservations for Amsterdam. Because psychedelics are legal in the Netherlands, this is where the Irish therapy group holds its retreats.

THE BOYS' CLUB: A PSYCHEDELIC JOURNEY THROUGH GRIEF

It's early afternoon at a retreat center an hour north of Amsterdam. A fierce October storm beats against the windows. It seems like a good day to be inside, to cozy up into our duvets and pillows, and to go on a six-hour psychedelic adventure.

There are seven of us ready to step into our unknowns, guided by three psychedelic therapists. I feel safe. Curious, but not anxious. My family and friends think I'm crazy for doing this.

"Do you know what you're getting into?" "Is this a little impulsive after all you've been through?"

No, I don't know exactly what I'm getting into, and it doesn't feel impulsive. Uncertain, but not rash.

In researching psychedelics and talking with the program's trained therapists, I found myself feeling, "Yes, yes, yes." Maybe this will help me feel something more than relief about Greg's death. Maybe this will help me process guilty feelings that I could have been more patient or attentive, especially during his last two years with psychotic dementia and all its paranoia and hallucinations.

I have no idea what the benefits or outcomes may be. But a part of me senses that I need this, so here I am, and here we go.

We each grind up the psilocybin truffles in our teacups. One of the facilitators pours hot water and ginger into our cups. We stir the "medicine," eat the ground truffles from the bottom of the teacup, and sip the hot water to wash them down.

The six-hour journey into our consciousness has begun.

I sit with my back to the wall and pull the duvet around my legs. Six other "journeyers" are spread across the retreat center room on their mats, preparing for their trips. We've traveled here from India, Hong Kong, Greece, Sweden, Switzerland, and the United States.

After I finish eating the magic mushrooms, I do feel some anxiety. I hope I don't have a bad trip. That the truffles won't make me vomit. That I'll be able to deal with whatever may come up.

My intention for today is twofold:

May I learn from sorrow and be transformed by it.
May I be open to love and creativity.

Oh, boy, it's time to unshackle my mind and let it take me wherever it wants to go. I will try to accept and understand what it wants to teach me.

After eating the truffles, we put on eye masks and get comfortable. The soundtrack begins, emanating from speakers in each corner of the room. The music sounds angry to me. Is this song from *Lord of*

the Rings? Sitting up feels uncomfortable. A six-hour trip? I lie down on my mat, fluff up the pillow, and tuck the duvet around me. My nest in the corner of the retreat center room feels secure.

Things start happening. Not abstract images and kaleidoscopes, but real action, like I'm in a film that defies a genre.

I wade through a dark, damp forest of ominous dark blue vines. They multiply around me. They try to catch me, block me, strangle me. I am lost and disoriented. The vines move and try to trap me in their slithering menace. It feels like this is the end. I am going to die here.

I break free from the vines and run to a dangerous-looking neighborhood of bars, strip clubs, and jails. It's like a combination of Dickens's dark, decaying, poverty-stricken London and sleazy New York Times Square in the 1970s. There are so many alleyways with dead ends. Where should I go?

A red neon light blinks on and off at a sleazy joint called Evil. A character with dark, slicked-back, greasy hair and pock-marked skin calls to me from the door of the bar.

"Come in. You know you want to be here. This is where you want to be."

"I'm not evil. I don't want to be evil. Leave me alone. Where am I?"

"Hell, my dear. You have died and come to us. Welcome to hell."

"No! I don't belong here. I did my best. I did everything I could do. I want to live. I don't want to be in hell. Please let me go."

"Good luck with that," Mr. Evil sneers.

I fight to get out of the warren of menacing alleyways. I am out of breath from running from one dead end to another. I don't deserve this. I want to live. How do I get out? I want to live, damn it.

There's a flight of well-lit, wide stairs at the end of an alley. I run up the stairs two at a time, push open the heavy fire alarm door, and escape onto what looks like Lincoln Center in New York. I step into a bright, wide-open piazza. Hundreds of people applaud as I step out. (The applause was from the program's soundtrack. What a weird coincidence that it played as I escaped.)

I cry. I laugh. "I'm alive. Oh God, I am alive. I'm not in hell!" I yank off the duvet and throw my arms up. "I am alive. I am alive."

Glittering globes of silver and gold jewels float overhead as I walk through the piazza. Tiaras and necklaces are handed to me.

"I'm not a fine jewelry person."

"Perhaps you might change your mind," says a kind voice from the ether.

I keep walking and start to see boats. Little Boston Whalers. Water taxis. Island ferries. Decadent yachts with heliports.

Phew. I must be close to home. I must be back in Rhode Island. I'm almost back to where I belong.

But no.

I enter a town square and see my beloved friend, Jimma, who died eighteen years ago.

"JIMMA!" I screech with joy. Tears clog my eye mask, and I try to breathe. "I can't believe I get to see you again. Oh, Jimma, we miss you so much."

He laughs, pushes his glasses up his nose, and fondly says, "Fuckin' Lois. What are you doing here?"

"I've lost Greg. He's not in hell. Will you help me find him? Will you take care of him for me?"

"Chill, chill. Of course, I will."

I rush to give Jimma some messages from the real world as I don't know how long I'll be here.

"Jimma, Mary misses you so much. She still has your favorite UNH shirts. Jeff's a teacher and married another teacher, a beautiful woman from Concord."

"A beautiful, smart woman? Go, Jeff."

Before I can update him on the rest of his family, we see Greg. He's walking around aimlessly. Kind of cruising the scene, taking it all in. He has no walker, no tremors, no Parkinson's disease. He looks forty, with a runner's body, wearing his tight brown leather pants and a University of Miami T-shirt. He is magnificent. I run to him.

I can't hear what Greg says because I'm sobbing. My body heaves and shakes. My heart races. It's hard to breathe. I have never wept like this in the conscious world. My chest hurts, my body is burning. I throw off the duvet. I breathe in but find it hard to exhale. I can't breathe.

I feel the presence of Rob, one of the therapists. He gently lays a hand on top of my head and another on my chest. I hold onto his hand.

"Breathe, breathe. I'm so sorry you're going through this, Lois, but you must keep going. The medicine is working. Breathe in and let out how you feel. Yes, make a noise as you exhale. Let it go. Feel it and let it go."

Rob shows me how to express my despair. I growl, shout, and groan. The despair feels suffocating.

"I did my best," I say, weeping. "I tried so hard. I tried so hard. I am so, so tired."

The music is lighter and more playful. I see Greg and Jimma shooting the shit. Through my weeping snot, I burst out laughing at the two of them.

"We're OK. Stop worrying. You know you worry too much," they both say.

I weep more. Two men I loved, a husband, and a best friend I met the first week of college. They're with me. They're healthy, having a good time, and they seem so happy. I feel safe and relieved.

My vagina burns. Do I have a yeast infection? A UTI? Should I ask a facilitator to help me to the bathroom? This is uncomfortable.

I remember the advice from our prejourney prep session. "You may experience uncomfortable bodily sensations. Be curious about them. What might they be telling you?"

"I just need some antibiotics," I say aloud.

The vagina throbs. My first love from college appears.

What is this? Lois's Psychedelic Boys' Club? Why is my trip filling up with men I loved? This is not what I expected.

Greg shakes hands with Dave, my first lover. They hit it off immediately. Oh, these two handsome, intelligent men; men whom women liked to throw themselves at.

They are yucking it up, like lifelong friends, although they met just a few minutes ago.

"Hey, you two assholes. Who gave me the STD? Is this why my vagina aches?"

They laugh, and so do I. Who would have thought a burning vagina, and an STD would show up on a sixty-eight-year-old woman's psychedelic trip?

"Maybe your vagina is burning because you see us," they laugh.

They go to a bar, order beers, and start talking about me. They don't know I can hear their conversation.

"Why your deep connection with Lois?"

"She got me, even the broken parts. She was tender and loved my insecure, overly sensitive self. I could be who I am with her. She also inspired me to be a better version of myself. And her energy just lights up life."

"She loved me despite my emotional insecurities too. She didn't want the male macho thing, and she got annoyed when I tried to run away from how I felt. It was so easy being with her. You could always trust Lois in every way."

"But sometimes she could be a handful, right?"

"Came with the package. An exuberant spirit can't be contained and is never predictable. As frustrating as she could be sometimes, I wish I had shown up and cared for her better. I withdrew too much into my insecurities and left her alone too much. I didn't mean to abandon her emotionally."

"Same here. I taught her what ghosting meant before ghosting was even a thing. What a pathetic lesson. How could I have done that to her?"

So why didn't you tell me that? Why did we suppress so much? Why did I put up with so much? Why couldn't you—or we—have been more honest with one another? Why did we run from difficult, deep conversations?

Jimma walks over. "I never understood your attraction to those two. But I kind of get it now. They saw your magical energy."

"There was a mystical spiritual connection, too, Jimma. I accepted some of their human flaws because of that mysterious energy between us. There was a tender love. And you're right, I never should have put up with so much. What a gift to understand this."

Wait, where am I now? How did I get on this New York water taxi with my dear friend, Bob, and my son, Ian? More guys

I love. Unbelievable. This really is The Boys' Club Psychedelic Trip.

We've just come from the "Bodies" exhibit at the South St. Seaport, where Bob and Ian marveled that there are twenty thousand fine-touch nerve endings in a penis.

As we pass Governor's Island on the water taxi, Bob tells Ian about its history. Ian laps up Bob's fascinating facts.

"Excuse me, sir," a passenger on the boat says to Bob. "I think you have your facts wrong."

We laugh hilariously. So much for "Professor" Bob.

On my mat, I am belly laughing. I shout into the retreat room, "Thank you, Bob. I love you, Ian."

It dawns on me that Jimma and Bob helped us raise Ian. They showed Ian a man can be vulnerable, kind, generous, playful, fearful, disappointed, and sad. Sometimes all at the same time.

This realization triggers another snot-filled crying rage; they are sobs of gratitude. So many love me and encourage me, even if some are dead. The love is everlasting.

Ian pops in. "Hi, Mom. You're doing great. I told you you'd like psychedelics."

"This is too hard, Ian. You didn't tell me it would be so difficult."

"Just relax, Mom. Remember when you always wanted to hold my hand crossing the streets In New York? I'll hold your hand now. You don't have to be the one taking care of everyone."

Then Ian is gone.

I hear Bob's voice again. "I don't like this at all. Are you sure you're OK?" Oh, my Bob, who has always been there for me since junior high school.

I am not OK, but I can't stop. The medicine has me in its grip.

"Hey, you guys. I want to think about something else now during this psychedelic trip. It's time to move on," I say aloud.

"Oh, no you don't. Today's our day. We never got enough of you. You were always so busy."

Greg and I talk about the last few hours of his conscious life and how we yelled at each other

"I could have been nicer at the end. I am so sorry for not being more patient," I say during the waning time of this psychedelic journey.

"It was the Parkinson's, not me. I wished I could have been a better husband. You did the best you could. I never would have had such a good life without you."

My body is spent. I put my hands on my chest and take big breaths in and out. I am drenched from sweat, snot, and saliva. Yes, I am learning from my sorrow, but does it need to be this hard? My body aches. I am depleted. How much longer?

I overhear Greg and Jimma talking about Dave.

"Maybe she should get together with him. He's still alive. He might be a breath of fresh air for her," says Greg.

Wise Jimma thinks about this for a few minutes. "I don't know. Maybe Lois should relax for a while and make no decisions. Maybe he was hanging with us because she's grieving love that is over. Today, Lois is making peace with letting us go."

Jimma died unexpectedly, alone on the beach. Greg lost consciousness before I could say a final goodbye. Dave disappeared. But today, I have been able to say goodbye to all of them. Thank you, thank you for this day.

I sense the journey is coming to an end. I hear the ukulele rendition of "Somewhere Over the Rainbow" by Israel Kamakawiwo'ole.

Someday I'll wish upon a star
Wake up where the clouds are far behind me
Where trouble melts like lemon drops
High above the chimney top, that's where
You'll find me

"Thank you, guys," I shout into the room, brimming with happiness. "Thank you, thank you. I am reclaiming my exuberant spirit. Thank you for loving me and thank you for us. I am so happy to be alive."

I am wrung out and filled with love. So much love.

GOODBYE TO THAT WOMAN

Before flying home from the retreat, I go to dinner in Amsterdam and meet the woman I used to be. Or, more accurately, that I had aspired to be.

A corporate-looking woman in her fifties sits alone at a table next to mine. A loud American couple behind us is telling the waiter about the great meals they have had during their European vacation. They brag about Michelin restaurants and make sure the waiter knows they are wealthy orthopedic surgeons from Atlanta.

They sound like the worst version of ugly Americans. I wonder what they look like.

I try to discreetly turn my head to get a look at them. The woman next to me does the same. We catch each other eavesdropping and burst out laughing.

No wonder many Europeans can't stand Americans, I think to myself.

We decide to eat together.

SLOW LOSS

She is a woman of renown, a former CEO, and a sought-after advisor. She has just flown into Amsterdam to give a keynote speech after selling her European vacation home.

"We never used the villa. It was a dream. Yet, it was sad to sell it."

"What happened to the dream?" I ask.

"My husband has been dying for fourteen years of a rare cancer."

"Oh, how difficult for you. My husband recently died after twelve years with Parkinson's."

"What's difficult for me is that I was ready for my husband to die but because of a new immunotherapy treatment, he's going to live."

We burst into laughter again. We are having so much fun, this sick humor among two women caregivers. After so many years of a husband's decline, you start to imagine what life might be like after he dies. A life free of responsibilities, doctors' appointments, planning around him, and worry over what crisis might happen next.

"What are you doing now?" I ask.

"I've been trying to finish a book, but I've lost interest in it, even though I spent two years traveling around the world to do interviews and research."

"Your soul's just not into it?"

"Exactly. The project is important, but I'm stuck."

Our conversation moves to U.S. issues that she has been deeply and personally affected by.

"Why don't you write about that," I suggest. "The passion and vulnerability in your voice makes me think this is something you want to explore.

"Maybe," she says unconvincingly and then changes the subject. "What are you doing in Amsterdam?"

"A psilocybin psychedelic retreat."

"Get out. I've always wanted to do that, especially after reading Michael Pollan's *How to Change Your Mind* book. What got you interested in it?"

"I'm always curious about emerging trends. And I just had a sense that psychedelics could help me. For years, I've felt adrift and out of touch with the real me. Not just because of my husband's disease and needs. I've worked so hard all my life to be seen as successful, competent, and brave. But I've never felt comfortable with how I was defining success for myself. Something felt off."

"Like imposter syndrome?"

"Not that as much as just not feeling like I was showing up as the real me."

"What was your trip like?"

"It was exhausting. I'm just beginning to process it, but it feels like I've had a big shift. I realize that those who love me, love me for my spirit and my creative, messy, exuberant energy. The bravery they love has nothing to do with my professional identity. I was obsessed with my career and how I was perceived. The trip helped me see that my busy life was a kind of hell. It kept me from prioritizing my relationships or believing in my creativity. Or just feeling light and free."

She nods. She's younger than me but of the age where women had to fight the alpha male culture to be taken seriously. We worked so hard and missed so much.

"What do you want to do next?" she asks.

"I want to feel light, be playful, slow it all down, have no expectations, just go with what feels right."

"Is that all?"

We laugh. We know unwinding and trusting our inner selves is daunting.

We exchange numbers. A car is waiting outside for her.

"Thanks for telling me about your psychedelic experience. I'm going to explore it. It's something I've been interested in for a while."

"Do it! It was one of the most important things I've done for myself."

I walk back to my hotel full of gratitude. What a lovely woman and an interesting conversation.

Thank God, I'm not her. Twenty years ago, I wanted to be a well-known and respected person like her. Phew.

I am free from having to live up to a public persona.

I am free to write books like this, exposing the messy realness of my life.

I am free to live life like it is a giant experiment.

I am free to go on a psychedelic retreat and rid myself of emotional insecurities.

I am free of guilt that I could have done a better job caring for my husband.

I am free to be a silly wood nymph flitting around parties, wearing ivy wreaths and sparkling crystals.

I am not yet free from uncertainty. What will emerge next in my life? Who am I now? What should I do or not do when I get home?

The only thing I feel certain about is that I should trust my soul, the soul that guided me through the psychedelic trip. She's the niggling inner voice that's always right. The voice that is our hunch, our instinct, our compass. When we ignore her and things don't go well, we say, "Damn, I should have listened to that little inner voice."

I'm also listening to Greg's cousin's voice. During the Big Fat Portuguese Death Vigil, she said, "When this is all over, you should do whatever you want."

Okey-dokey.

What I want is slow and easy. Few commitments. No "shoulds." The wide-open space to be spontaneous. The strength to say no.

For our first Christmas without Greg, I went to LA to visit Ian and his partner, Ava. I flew first class. It made travel so easy.

Was that ticket reckless spending? Maybe. My former self, my money-fraidy-cat self, would have been full of guilt. But I am no longer her, and I have decided to do something radical for a year—something that I thought was impossible for me.

I've decided not to worry about money and take Greg's cousin's advice to do whatever I want. Slow and easy guide my decisions. Not how much does it cost or will the money last.

I meet with my financial advisor.

"Now that you've settled Greg's finances and sold the house, what's your budget? What do you need to live on?" he asks.

"There is no budget. For a year, I'm doing and spending whatever I want. I'm going to enjoy my bereavement binge. Then we can look at things."

He doesn't say anything. This is not like me at all. I can see he wants to tell me not to be reckless, that I'm grieving and could make stupid decisions. I respect him more when he stays silent. Smart man.

Aside from that first-class ticket, I spend little. It turns out that slow and easy doesn't cost much money. There are no decisions to make about what to spend on house maintenance, business travel, work clothes, or doctors because there is no home, business, work, or doctors.

Becoming someone new is not a decision. It is a slow and easy evolution. It is a bereavement binge where I get to do whatever I want

SLOW LOSS

and see what happens. It is a time to feel impulsive hunches and try them out. To trust myself even when I feel adrift, which is more frequent than I'd like.

I'm not sure how long it will take for Tigger to get her bounces back, or whether I'll be able—or want to—bounce that high.

I'm not sure of a lot, and that is OK.

EGG FIGHTS AND ICE QUEENS

"You are losing it."

The egg yolks drip down the white cupboards. Shattered brown eggshells stick to the window over the sink.

"No, you are losing it. I can't take this anymore. You're giving money to strangers and getting way too involved in their dramas. My God, they think you actually know what you're talking about. The way you speak with such confidence and kindness. Do they have any idea? Maybe they do. Maybe they're using you, big time. This has to stop."

Minutes earlier, I opened the refrigerator, grabbed a carton of eggs, and threw ten eggs at him.

Bam, bam, bam.

Greg was too stunned to move.

This was not his calm, rational wife.

Our fights had never been hot, fiery, or physical. We preferred the icy freeze. One of us would glare in disgust and walk away. The silent tension would be as sharp and ominous as the giant icicles that hung from the roof's eaves in early March.

SLOW LOSS

What a mess.
The kitchen.
Our life.
His disease.
My unraveling.

Then I woke up. Good God, what a horrible dream. I thought I was over this.

During my psychedelic trip on the floor of the Amsterdam retreat center, I sobbed and screamed, "I did the best I could. I did the best I could. I'm so sorry. I am so, so sorry." The Greg in my trip reassured me his life would never have been as wonderful without me. He told me that it was time for me to keep living. To enjoy myself. To stop guilting myself.

And yet, I wonder.

Could I have been more patient? Was I kind enough?

Should I have thrown eggs and broken furniture instead of building an igloo around myself? An igloo that froze most reactions to his erratic behavior, hallucinations, and demented accusations. An igloo that I thought would protect my sanity.

An igloo that turned me into a high-functioning ice queen who navigated one day and then the next. An ice queen that held my heart hostage. An ice queen who froze all feelings to persevere as a long-haul caregiver.

I don't want to remember yelling at him during his last conscious hours before the hospice ambulance arrived.

I don't want to remember the last four years of his disease or write about this anymore. Enough, enough, enough.

I want the dreams to stop.
My pen to run out.
The grief to thaw.

A FATTY BETRAYAL

The creamy green soup took two hours to cook. I carefully poured the cooked onions, leeks, garlic, shallots, celery, broccoli, spinach, and peas into the blender, gave it a whir, and poured the green puree back into the pot. I added another cup of peas to give the soup some texture. The finishing touch is a pint of heavy cream.

Do I need to wait for dinnertime to feast on my favorite soup and naan bread? No, I do not. I can do whatever I want.

I eat a large bowl of soup and go back for seconds. It's delicious and loaded with nutrients.

It's also going to kill me.

Within an hour, the stomach cramps kick in. Worse than ever. This new lactose intolerance thing is cruel. As is not being able to eat fatty foods, chocolate, or drink alcohol.

My digestive system is a tyrant, locking me up in some kind of Food Guantanamo, torturing me for my years of eating any damned thing I wanted. Or maybe it's just bad luck. Or did years of worry ruin my stomach?

SLOW LOSS

Ice cream, grilled cheese and tomato, cheesecake, salmon, lamb, macaroni and cheese, brownies with hot fudge, ice cream, and whipped cream.

Thanks to my inherited genes, I've never had to worry about being fat. I ate chocolate chip ice cream after dinner every night. Drank creamy coffee and ice cream frappes. Scooped more raw brownie mix into my mouth than into the baking pan. On Friday nights Greg and I had special dinners: a fondue or a simple pate, brie, apple, and crusty bread treat. Always with good wine from Greg's wine store.

"You're in such great shape," a guy recently told me. "What do you do?"

Was he expecting me to talk about tennis, running, hiking, or bicycling up Alpine mountains?

"Lucky genes," I say.

If I had been honest, I would have said, "I'm bereft and don't know what to eat since my favorite foods have betrayed me. That's why I'm thin."

No alcohol, either. Whatever enzymes digest Veuve Clicquot, Cloudy Bay sauvignon blanc, and the French Burgundies I inherited from my husband are MIA. They refuse to do their job.

Fucking inconsiderate assholes. Why have you deserted me? Why now when I could use some treats?

I explain these woes to a gastroenterologist, hoping there's an easy fix. Pills? Rip out my gallbladder?

"I am so sorry. You just have to avoid these foods and alcohol. If you eat them, you're sick. If you avoid them, you're a very healthy woman for your age."

Last Thursday, I snapped. I ordered a Neapolitan pizza with anchovies at the neighborhood Italian restaurant. And two glasses

A FATTY BETRAYAL

of an Austrian Gruner Veltliner. I ate the entire pizza. It may have been the best pizza I have ever eaten.

My blood pressure spiked thirty points. My racing heart and night sweats crushed me. Some sixty-eight-year-olds might think they were having a heart attack. The recent MRI of my arteries shows they're in tip-top shape despite a life of luscious fat and free fine wine.

I want fat.

I want a little fat in my face to iron out the wrinkles.

I want some fat in my flat ass so my bathing suit bottom doesn't sag.

I want fat for its substance, richness, and ability to make other ingredients sing.

Sigh.

Yesterday, I turned off the wine refrigerator that came with the apartment and packed up my mother's martini glasses, which can double as pot du crème dishes.

This letting go is a bitch.

LIVING IN THE LAND OF LIMINALITY

I am no longer waiting.

Waiting in TSA lines to travel to clients' corporate headquarters, to speaking gigs, to conferences about everything and nothing.

Waiting for budget approvals.

Waiting for the alarm clock to ring.

Waiting to be free from financial worries.

Waiting to move back to the city.

Waiting for my son to be on his feet, deeply alive in his adulthood.

Waiting for my husband's difficult life to end.

Waiting to know what I'm supposed to be doing with life.

I'm living in the Land of Liminality. It's such a foreign place.

There are no street signs, and neither Google Maps nor Waze works. Gurus, experts, and the overly confident are banned.

Planes are unnecessary. Walking, strolling, and wandering are how you get around, transporting you to nowhere in particular.

There are stop signs. Not the red and demanding kind. They're more like quiet reminders that you can stop doing what you don't want to do. That in the Land of Liminality being lost is a good thing. That uncertainty is a necessary thing.

The definition of liminality, from the Latin word for threshold, is being between the old world we've left behind and a new world where we've not yet arrived. It is characterized by uncertainty, instability, and ambiguity, as well as by creativity, possibility, and transformation.

Being lost in the Land of Liminality is like floating, head laying back in the salt water with my face to the sky on an eighty-two-degree summer day, letting the soft waves of the protected Cape Cod bay rock me, knowing I'm safe from the dangerous, crashing waves and undertows of wide-open oceans like the North Sea.

There's a noble quiet in the Land of Liminality. There's a reverence that we need to let go of what once was and who we were. Liminality encourages us not to fear uncertainty, and to be excited about who we are becoming. Even if what that means is unclear.

No rushing. No expectations.

Some days, I cross over to Old Reality because I think the familiar will make me feel better, more grounded, clear, and in control. Yet I feel ornery there. Frustrated, out of place, not myself. I return, realizing I can no longer live within the boundaries of Old Reality.

And so, I wander the wide-open spaces of Liminality.

I notice the architecture.

I notice that there are fewer trees. Their rarity makes me appreciate them more. Their vivid green against the city's cold concrete buildings. Their roots burst up under the sidewalk pavement in defiance of those who don't respect that growth can't be controlled.

I notice I sleep soundly despite the traffic, the loud, pulsing music emanating from cars stopped at red lights, and the brawls that break out after last call at Murphy's Irish bar. It's all so alive.

LIVING IN THE LAND OF LIMINALITY

I notice reflections in windows, street art, the angle of the winter sun at 4:00 p.m., peoples' shoes, and how they walk during a snowstorm.

I notice how delicious my morning coffee tastes.

I notice that the night sweats are gone.

I notice how good my back feels when I relax horizontally on the couch to read, nap, and wonder.

There's no deadline for leaving the Land of Liminality. Previous residents tell me that I'll know when to move on.

What's next, they say, will be sweet and juicy, like biting into the first Macoun apple of the season from Phantom Farms.

You'll be surprised, they assure me. The more you give in to sacred Liminality, the more you will marvel at what's next. Who you are meant to be, how you are meant to live, and who you are meant to love and be loved by.

I put my face up to the pale winter sun and soak in just a hint of warmth.

I am a wanderer in the Land of Liminality. Not waiting for anything.

Just slowly moving onward.

ACKNOWLEDGMENTS

What saved me and gave me hope during the very worst times of Greg's disease were family and friends who showed up without being asked. Friends who knew that things were not OK, even when I so confidently assured them that everything was fine. Friends who knew that a person in crisis doesn't have the energy or wherewithal to know how to ask for support or what kind of help to ask for.

Thank you to my sisters Nancy Kelly, Norene Pavilon, and Susan Purinai for bossing around their bossypants older sister, and doing so with such compassion, consistency, and selflessness. Special thanks to Nancy, a wise geriatric nurse practitioner who helped me understand complex medical issues, ask the right questions, and make difficult decisions. I love you, dear sisters.

My brother Jim Kelly and his wife Sarah showed up unannounced on the morning Greg and I were moving from our house of thirty-eight years. They directed the movers, brought food, set up Greg's bedroom so he could sleep through the chaos, measured for grab bars and extra stair railings, and came back a few days later to install everything. They, also, with brother-in-law Tom Pavilon, cleaned out Greg's assisted living apartment under a tight deadline. You guys are the best.

Maria DeCarvahlo and I held each other as we grieved together about losing our husbands, bit by bit, over so many years. Some days, we laughed at the inanities of our husbands' dementia; it was more healing than sobbing. Maria made us dinner reservations, recommended books and television series, asked evocative questions that expanded my perspective and challenged my assumptions, urged me to research assisted living options before a crisis, brought lunch with linen napkins and fine china to the hospice, and much more. Maria's greatest gift: helping me see how to grow and expand amid loss. Maria, you are extraordinary: a giver, a learner, and a seeker of meaning.

Soon after Greg's PD diagnosis, Pat Gifford invited me to join a monthly support group she belonged to for wives of husbands with PD. This was a sacred group where we could share everything, ask anything, or just show up and know that we were not alone in the bizarre and unpredictable world of PD. The upside of PD was becoming friends with these intelligent, compassionate, and resilient women: Pat Gifford, Carla Ricci, Petrina Babcock, Jody Bishop, Alice Benedict, Nancy Rozendahl, Jacqueline Ott, Joan Retsinas, Sarah Gleason, and Heidi Smith.

Thank you to lifelong friends Bob Russo, Maura Kelly, and Mary Ellen Donald for calling or texting all the time, listening without judgment, and doing so with so much unconditional love.

To "Team UNH," how lucky are we to have one another? During difficult days, Greg gave me good advice: "You need to see your UNH friends." Our fifty-year friendship is full of laughter, caring, optimism, mischievousness, and love. No wonder people want to crash our reunions.

ACKNOWLEDGMENTS

Special thanks to UNHer Yvonne Richard, who read a draft of the book, saw that the working title didn't capture its essence, and helped create a new title and positioning for this book. What a gift.

To the talented and spiritual team of psychedelic therapists at Inwardbound, thank you for helping me do the hard work of learning from my sorrow and rediscovering love and creativity.

During the last four years of Greg's life and the first year of widowhood, I logged into Zoom Monday through Friday to join writer/performer/teacher Ann Randolph and her Unmute writing community. Writing and experiencing others' writing was both transcendent and healing. Thank you to Ann and the community for such creative bravery and honest storytelling and for encouraging me to write this book. Writing every day with you saved my sanity.

Thanks to developmental editor Stuart Horwitz for wise and frank advice and to Susan Pohlman for her detailed copyediting. Good editors are good teachers. Both Stuart and Susan encouraged me to write more about the early years of my marriage so that readers could understand how much Greg and I loved one another. I can't yet remember those stories. In my relief, grief, and exhaustion, I can only remember my husband with advanced Parkinson's disease and all its difficult behavioral and cognitive changes. This omission is on me, not these talented editors.

When designer Molly Regan asked what feeling I wanted the book cover to convey, I showed her my collage of a joyous woman dancer and someone slogging through mud. She immediately understood that love, caregiving, and loss are full of defiant exuberance and messes. Thanks, Molly, for capturing so much in one book cover.

Lastly, to sons Ian Matta and Greg Frishman (did you think I had forgotten to mention you?): I see the best of your father in you and so much more. Dad's love for you made his last years bearable for him and for me. (However, his bragging about you may have been unbearable to some.) Special thanks for trusting and supporting me when I had to make difficult decisions and seeing the healing power of psychedelics. Psychonauts, unite.

ABOUT THE AUTHOR

Lois Kelly grew up in Boston and has lived in Rhode Island for forty-three years. She graduated from the University of New Hampshire and was a speechwriter, keynote speaker, and corporate communications and marketing strategist. She is the author of several books, including *Rebels at Work: A Handbook for Leading Change from Within* and *Be the Noodle: 50 Ways to be a Compassionate, Courageous, Crazy-Good Caregiver*. Her late husband, Greg Matta, urged Lois and their sons, Greg Jr. and Ian, to believe in their aspirations and talents, take risks, and stay real.

I hope you enjoyed reading *Slow Loss*. If you did, I'd really appreciate it if you could take a couple of minutes to leave a quick review or rating for the book on Amazon, Goodreads, or your preferred book site.

Reviews from readers mean so much to authors like me in getting the word out about our books. Even just a brief comment or a star rating would make a big difference and be incredibly helpful.

I'm deeply grateful for readers like you.

Lois

www.ingramcontent.com/pod-product-compliance
Lightning Source LLC
Chambersburg PA
CBHW020419010526
44118CB00010B/331